D1515106

MASTERING DIGITAL RESEARCH

A GUIDE FOR STUDENTS

First Canadian Edition

DISCARDED
NO LONGER THE
PROPERTY OF GBC

BONNIE L. TENSEN
Seminole Community College

KEITH HAMPSON
Ryerson University

Casa Loma Library
George Brown College

NELSON EDUCATION

JUN 7 2013

NELSON EDUCATION

Mastering Digital Research: A Guide for Students, First Canadian Edition
by Bonnie L. Tensen and Keith Hampson

Associate Vice President, Editorial Director:
Evelyn Veitch

Editor-in-Chief, Higher Education:
Anne Williams

Executive Editor:
Laura Macleod

Marketing Manager:
Amanda Henry

Developmental Editor:
Theresa Fitzgerald

Photo Researcher and Permissions Editor:
Sandra Mark

Content Production Manager:
Susan Wong

Production Service:
Pre-PressPMG

Copy Editor:
Kelli Howey

Proofreader:
Mark Mayell

Indexer:
Shan Young

Production Coordinator:
Ferial Suleman

Design Director:
Ken Phipps

Managing Designer:
Katherine Strain

Interior Design:
Jennifer Leung

Cover Design:
Johanna Liburd

Cover Image:
©iStockphoto.com/Daniel Gilbey

Compositor:
Pre-PressPMG

Printer:
Webcom

COPYRIGHT © 2010
by Nelson Education Ltd.

Adapted from *Research Strategies for a Digital Age*, Second Edition, by Bonnie L. Tensen, published by Thomson Wadsworth. Copyright ©2007 by Thomson Wadsworth.

Printed and bound in Canada
1 2 3 4 12 11 10 09

For more information contact Nelson Education Ltd., 1120-Birchmount Road, Toronto, Ontario, M1K 5G4. Or you can visit our Internet site at http://www.nelson.com

Statistics Canada information is used with the permission of Statistics Canada. Users are forbidden to copy this material and/or redisseminate the data, in an original or modified form, for commercial purposes, without the expressed permissions of Statistics Canada. Information on the availability of the wide range of data from Statistics Canada can be obtained from Statistics Canada's Regional Offices, its World Wide Web site at <http://www.statcan.gc.ca>, and its toll-free access number 1-800-263-1136.

ALL RIGHTS RESERVED. No part of this work covered by the copyright herein may be reproduced, transcribed, or used in any form or by any means—graphic, electronic, or mechanical, including photocopying, recording, taping, Web distribution, or information storage and retrieval systems—without the written permission of the publisher.

For permission to use material from this text or product, submit all requests online at www.cengage.com/permissions. Further questions about permissions can be emailed to permissionrequest@cengage.com

Every effort has been made to trace ownership of all copyrighted material and to secure permission from copyright holders. In the event of any question arising as to the use of any material, we will be pleased to make the necessary corrections in future printings.

Library and Archives Canada Cataloguing in Publication

Tensen, Bonnie L Mastering digital research: a guide for students/ Bonnie L. Tensen, Keith Hampson.— 1st Canadian ed.

Includes index.
ISBN 978-0-17-644002-2

1. Electronic information resource searching—Textbooks. 2. Internet research—Textbooks. I. Hampson, Keith Christopher, 1961– II. Title.

ZA3075.T45 2009
001.4'202854678   C2009-900239-6

13-ISBN: 978-0-17-644002-2
10-ISBN: 0-17-644002-X

Contents

Preface

"The Internet is revolutionary, but not Utopian."

ANDREW SHAPIRO ET AL., *Principles of Technorealism*

Research in a Digital Age

Many of today's students are masters at Internet "research." Having grown up with the web, they can quickly find and download a ringtone of the current number-one hit, obtain the lowest airfare for a weekend getaway to Montreal, or discover on Facebook whether or not that cutie they just met is unattached. It's not surprising, then, that they often approach scholarly research with great confidence (sometimes even disdaining the advice of teachers whom they perceive as "technochallenged"). They've come to believe that no information is beyond reach of their broadband connections. The world is rapidly becoming Internet proficient—even Internet dependent—and students are often on the leading edge of the digital learning curve.

But we've discovered that guidance on using the web for research is just as necessary today as in the past. This is one of the paradoxes of the Internet. While it has made more information easily accessible to more students, it has also made it easier for students to carry out poor research by, for example, making it easier to locate and use inaccurate information and plagiarizing.

The aim of this book is to teach students the following:

- Basic research strategies and library skills that will enable them to proficiently use online catalogues and databases to locate credible sources in modern college/university libraries

- Researching and evaluative skills that will enable them to identify reliable and academically appropriate information on the web

- Proper methods of incorporating and documenting these resources in their research papers (see <www.digitalresearch.nelson.ca>)

How This Book Is Organized

The idea for this text arose from my experiences teaching research and composition. My initial inclination was to focus to help students learn how to use research tools, such as library databases. Given their increased access to information, I expected that they would locate sources that were fair, accurate, and scholarly. Instead, the resources they referenced were often personal web pages containing biased or unsupported opinion, short newspaper or popular magazine articles written by journalists rather than experts, and abstracts of articles (instead of the articles themselves). Many of my students had advanced Internet surfing skills, but they lacked research acumen. I realized that the ability to use the new research tools needed to be matched with basic research skills. Technological ability is now inseparable from information literacy—at least when it comes to writing post-secondary-level papers that require research.

Mastering Digital Research: A Guide for Students is divided into three sections. The first section explains a process for beginning and sustaining a research project. Students are instructed how to use the online library catalogue as a starting point to learn:

- The basics of creating matching terms and search phrases (e.g., keyword and Boolean phrases)
- The art of using scholarly sources as leads to locate other valuable scholarly sources
- The basics of evaluating sources of information to ensure that they are relevant, reliable, and unbiased

The search phrases students develop with the help of the online catalogue are then used to explore electronic databases (indices and collections of articles from popular and academic periodicals). We consider the distinctions between bibliographic and full-text databases (and the growing breed of databases that offer both types of results). It also includes instruction on how to use advanced search features to refine a search by more precisely delineating the types of sources required.

The second section of this text teaches students to use these same time-tested research strategies to cautiously explore the web—outside of library systems—first, by casting their research nets in "stocked ponds" (i.e., search engines, directories, and subject guides), and then by evaluating this information to confirm that it meets the stringent requirements of academic research. The section concludes with a chapter on field research (interviews and surveys), with suggestions about how to maximize use of the Internet to efficiently conduct these studies.

The final section of *Mastering Digital Research: A Guide for Students* begins with a comprehensive warning against plagiarizing. The Internet poses a dilemma for instructors as well as students. Most instructors list academic dishonesty among the top 5 challenges of teaching in higher education. The brief one- to two-paragraph-long admonition against plagiarism that appears in most handbooks is not sufficient to warn today's students. Most students find it very difficult to resist "borrowing" from the vast amount of text available to them on the web, and many more remain confused about what actually constitutes plagiarism. The text describes the many faces of plagiarism now made possible by the cut-and-paste nature of the World Wide Web and offers examples of improper paraphrasing and summarizing.

The text is supported by greatly expanded sections on documentation, posted on the companion website to this book (<www.digitalresearch.nelson.com>). Many instructors and students indicated that the documentation materials are extremely helpful, since they offer examples of the types of sources that students really use in their research projects (i.e., articles from databases and web pages). Therefore, these sections have been expanded and now feature the most current information on how to document conventional print sources as well as the new types of electronic resources available in school libraries. Documentation has become confusing because digital resources are constantly morphing into new forms. For instance, databases once exclusively packaged in CD-ROMs are now delivered over the Internet. This website offers the most up-to-date documentation models for the Modern Language Association (MLA), American Psychological Association (APA), Council of Science Editors (CSE), and The Chicago Manual of Style (CMS) formats. It includes sample student essays in each of these formats that offer marginal notations to explain the intricacies of in-text and works-cited documentation choices. The site includes an annotated sample literary-analysis research paper.

Mastering Digital Research: A Guide for Students is a unique text. Many guides to the Internet are available. This is not one of them. The ideal starting place for scholarly research has always been, and still is, the academic library; this text teaches students to maximize their use of the new technologies available in our online libraries as well as on the web. The research paper is a staple of many academic classes, yet most handbooks provide only a cursory explanation of the research process; this text offers a step-by-step progression that enables students to build researching and evaluative skills while introducing them to a variety of research tools. Proper documentation is fundamental to the research project, yet few handbooks or guides provide sufficient examples of the newer forms (e.g., websites, database articles) by which information is made available. This text provides an abundance of sample entries of the types of documents students are now using in four different styles. Most importantly, *Mastering Digital Research: A Guide for Students* is written to appeal to students and actively engage them in the research process.

Key Features of This Edition and Its Companion Website

- Examples of research strategies designed specifically for Canadian students
- Cautions against plagiarism that convey the importance of performing sound, ethical online research
- Extended examples of Works Cited entries of the types of resources that students are using
- Exercises for both online and on-campus courses, in recognition of the evolving nature of today's classroom
- Explanations of advanced search features to enable students to refine their searches using current search tools
- "Tip" boxes that reflect the most current Internet search tools
- "Writing Tips" that cover how to skillfully incorporate direct quotations
- Screenshots and examples that provide students with the most current technological information

- Extensive coverage of current MLA, APA, CSE, and CMS documentation styles, including new individual sections on CSE and CMS
- Sample research papers in CSE, CMS, and literary styles that demonstrate correct in-text and reference list documentation methods
- Citation directories on best practices in documentation that allow students to quickly locate instruction and examples for the type of source they're citing
- Simple, easy-to-navigate organization of topics
- Extensive web-based resources on proper documentation practices

If a course includes a research component, *Mastering Digital Research: A Guide for Students* is the perfect ancillary text that will help students develop research methods and habits that will serve them well throughout their academic careers.

Acknowledgments

I would like to thank my colleagues at SCC for the support and suggestions they have made so that this second edition could better address the needs of students. I also want to thank all those instructors whose feedback has aided me in making improvements. My thanks go to my students, as well, whose moments of confusion and enlightenment have helped me to find better ways to explain the strategies in this text. I'd also like to thank the folks at Wadsworth, Cengage Learning and Pre-Press Company, Inc. (especially Cheryl Forman, Jennifer Kostka, and Crystal Parenteau) for their support and help with this new edition. And I really can't find the words to thank Karen Kaivola for all the help she has given me in writing and in life (but when I do, I'm sure she'll help me edit them for greater clarity and impact).

—Bonnie L. Tensen

I wish to thank Laura Macleod of Nelson Education for her professionalism, inspiration, and friendship; and Theresa Fitzgerald for her consistent support and attention to detail. I'd also like to thank Anne Williams and Evelyn Veitch for their commitment to quality educational publishing. Special thanks go to the following reviewers, whose comments and criticisms have enriched the work: Paul Benedetti, University of Western Ontario; Scott Bunyan, Mohawk College; Angela Madden, Wilfrid Laurier University; and Linda McCloud-Bondoc, Athabasca University. Finally, I need to thank my family, Anne, Emma, and Claire, for being an endless source of laughter and joy.

–Keith Hampson

RESEARCH
BASICS

1

Defining the Topic of Your Research Paper

"The beginning is the most important part of the work."

PLATO, *The Republic*

Perhaps you will find no assignment more difficult than the research paper. After all, for most course assignments, your instructor provides the "raw materials" you need to success-fully complete the assignment (class readings, lectures, demonstrations, instructions). But the research paper requires you to strike out on your own: You must determine the topic (sometimes with little or no guidance), develop an approach that works for you, and base your claims and analysis on reliable information. Finally, after having expended much effort on these invisible but essential "behind-the-scenes" tasks, you must present your findings—accurately, cleverly, persuasively, and intelligently—in an essay, report, or argument. No wonder so many students find the research project daunting!

It is common for some students to minimize the amount of effort they put into the process of selecting and defining the topic of their research paper. However, if you have ever tried to write a detailed, informative, and well-supported essay without first focusing and thoroughly researching your topic—without really *knowing* what's important about that topic—you are already well aware of how difficult it is to sustain anything resembling an intelligent discussion beyond the first paragraph or two. Fortunately, there are tried-and-true methods that can help you get started. This chapter offers strategies for developing a topic that is both interesting and researchable. Later chapters will address how to develop an argument or analysis of that topic that is convincing and persuasive.

Determine the Degree of Freedom You Have for Topic Selection

Your first step is to gain a clear understanding of the degree of freedom you have to select and modify the topic of your research paper. Failure to follow the instructions provided by your instructor can lead to a poor grade, regardless of the quality of your work. If after thoroughly reviewing the assignment instructions you are still unsure, ask your instructor. Don't worry about approaching her; she will appreciate your desire to fully understand the requirements of the assignment.

Your freedom to choose the topic on which you are writing varies course-by-course. Some research projects have built-in parameters regarding both topic and method. For example, projects for a class in a specific discipline such as sociology, psychology, or biology will be about some aspect of the subject of the course itself. In some courses, the only requirement is that the subject must be researchable and "arguable." In this case the work of figuring out what exactly to write about is frequently left entirely up to you.

Because coming up with a good topic is often a real challenge, some students are most comfortable when instructors assign a specific subject to be researched. They prefer limited options. Others chafe at any restrictions and want to determine their own direction. Whichever group you fall into—whether you prefer more structure or greater freedom—the success of your project depends on your active involvement and interest.

Student-Selected Topics

When faced with a great deal of choice as to topic, it is a common mistake to choose a topic too quickly. The student chooses something currently in the news, something they think a research paper "should" address, or something they know other students are writing about. Starting a research paper in this manner rarely leads to a student's best work.

Below, I provide important tips for selecting a research topic that will save you time and improve the quality of your paper.

Approach Highly Controversial (and well-worn) Topics with Caution   Highly controversial topics should be avoided whenever possible. In my English I composition class, for example, I purposely make many of the most controversial topics (e.g., abortion, euthanasia, capital punishment, cloning, gun control, stem cell research) off limits. Whether or not your instructor does the same, I encourage caution about choosing these topics. There are three reasons for this:

1. Given the restrictions of most undergraduate research assignments, which generally require papers between 8 and 12 pages (or 2,000–3,000 words), a student would be hard-pressed to mount a convincing case about such complex and politicized topics. These are subjects that have been argued intensely in our society, often in polarizing ways, and are still far from being resolved. Even a cursory review of the basic arguments would require more than 10 pages to be persuasive to a broad audience.

(You should always assume that your readers are educated people, many of whom will not automatically agree with your views or assumptions and who will therefore need to be persuaded by careful, reasoned argument rather than by emotional appeal or unsupported claims.) It is foolish to take on a project that is doomed from the start—and that is exactly what an argument that can never persuade is: doomed.

2. It is all too easy to fall into "groupthink" when dealing with controversial issues. Rather than encouraging you to acquire information to formulate your own unique perspective on the issue, such papers tend to rehearse well-established and "safe" opinions. They simply put forth the "party line," whether from a conservative or progressive point of view, avoiding the hard work of original analysis.

3. Most students who choose one of these highly controversial topics do not really feel a compelling need to learn more about it. They already know what they think—or at least they think they do. Thus, in the end, their papers are often reiterations of what others have written before (or, worse, what they've heard on talk radio or seen on television) rather than any sustained engagement that leads to fresh insights.

Discover a Topic You Want to Know More About If you care about the topic on which you are writing it is highly likely that you will do better work. If there is a personal or professional reason why you want to learn about the subject, the process of researching and writing the paper will be less taxing on you and will you typically bring more energy and enthusiasm to the effort. Moreover, it's virtually impossible to make a reader care about a topic if you don't care about it yourself. And even if readers are interested before they start reading your essay, if your writing does not express a personal enthusiasm they will soon lose interest.

Example

- ***Whenever possible, research a topic that is personally relevant***

  A few years ago, one of my students wrote one of the worst research papers I have ever received. It argued that the laws regulating the age at which you can begin to drink alcohol should be lowered. The subject itself is a worthy one (over the years I have received numerous convincing essays that have argued this same point), but this particular essay offered no factual evidence or justification, and it was composed entirely of unsupported (and illogical) conjecture. As I discussed these problems with the student, it became apparent that he had absolutely no interest in the topic. He had chosen it because he thought I would find it fascinating. I don't usually allow students to abandon their research projects in the middle of the semester, but I made an exception in this case. In the end, the student produced a meticulously researched essay on methods for conserving the lobster population. His family is in the lobster business, and the diminishing crustacean population is a real threat to their livelihood. The student's research skills blossomed once he discovered a topic he truly cared about.

If you are finding it difficult to identify a topic that interests you, try stimulating your thinking by making a list of things in your own everyday life that "tick you off." Frustration is a strong emotion that can be redirected into more productive channels; you can use it to energize your desire to know more about a topic. Of course, not everything on your list will prove to be an appropriate topic for an academic paper. That's okay. The point of the exercise is to free you to generate ideas. With a little more creative/analytical thought, it is surprising how many times at least one of these "annoyances" can be transformed into an interesting, engaging, and researchable project.

Example

- ***Turning a "pet peeve" into a great research topic***

   A student listed as one of her pet peeves the fact that movie theatres charge $3.00 for a 500-mL bottle of water. In revisiting her list, she initially dismissed movie theatre snack prices as an unpromising topic for a research paper. But then she started thinking about the topic from a slightly different angle. Why was she willing to pay for something that is free at the theatre drinking fountain? The student was a confirmed bottled water drinker, convinced that bottled water is somehow healthier for her, but suddenly she found herself questioning things that she had never considered before. Where does bottled water come from? What is in bottled water? Is it healthier than tap water? Are there any significant differences between brands of bottled water? In this way, an idea that seemed like a dead end at first triggered an idea that led her to examine the nature of bottled water—a study that shattered many of her initial assumptions, and that has recently become the focus of increasing public scrutiny across North America.

Needless to say, if you are not invested in the topic, you will find it difficult to sustain an attitude that will energize and encourage you throughout the process. That lack of passionate involvement also will be obvious to your readers—who will, in turn, feel less interest than they would otherwise.

Instructor-Selected Topics

In many courses the instructor will assign specific research topics or place significant restrictions on your choice of topics. In these instances, it is still important (and possible) to make the topic your own. The trick is to find an angle or perspective on the topic that makes it come alive for you.

Adapting Instructor-Selected Topics   To make a prescribed topic interesting you can adapt the topic so that you want to know more. Ideally, you'll discover that the assignment provides an opportunity for you to learn more about the world, yourself, other people, and/or other cultures. Coming up with your own angle on a topic is simply a matter of learning how to ask good questions—and, of course, of knowing what interests you.

Example

- *Adapting Assigned Topics to Suit Your Interests*

    A student in a history course was assigned a research project on "The role of Canadian military in 20th-century international conflicts." Her first reaction was to dismiss this topic as essentially boring—she thought it might be of interest to a political science student, but not to her. But she can approach the topic in a way that suits her. For instance, if she is interested in film or the arts, she might compare the different ways military conflicts have been represented in feature films. If she is a sociology student, she could investigate the reasons why popular opinion concerning military initiatives has changed during the 20th century. If she is a student of economics, she might consider how the changing economic conditions and access to key resources, such as oil, might have influenced Canadian military practices. In the end, it all comes back to knowing yourself and making connections that initially might not seem obvious. Even if a research assignment at first seems mind-numbingly boring, you can find a way to transform it into a subject you care about.

QUICK CHECK

Make Your Project Relevant to You

Ask yourself the following questions:

- How does this topic relate to past/present concerns in my life?

- How does this subject relate to issues I have recently been studying or thinking about?

- How might this subject be important to me in the future?

- How can I use this subject to explore something that I want to know more about?

Getting Stuck: What If I Still Can't Think of a Good Topic?

If you're like most people, there will be times when you still cannot come up with a good topic. That is a perfectly normal (if not particularly pleasant) experience. After all, a research project involves multiple tasks, each of which is complex, and only some of which are tangible features of the final product. In the inevitable moments of frustration—moments common to experienced writers as well as novices—it helps to remember that good thinking rarely occurs in a vacuum. If you can't come up with a good topic on your own, seek aid elsewhere.

Getting Unstuck: Talk It Over

Help can come in various forms. One option is to discuss the project with others. Talking to someone is a great way to move beyond a mental block. Forcing yourself to articulate your thoughts (even if you still feel confused) can also lead to unexpected connections and surprising breakthroughs.

- Make an appointment with the course instructor. Explore your interests in conversation and ask for suggestions. Most instructors have many years of experience shaping ideas into great essays, and they will appreciate you making the effort to think through your essay. However, before you meet with your instructor, prepare your thoughts and share whatever notes you may have already generated. This will help you make the most of your time together.

- Discuss the project with another instructor in your school who teaches in the same subject or in one that is related to the subject area. As more and more interdisciplinary courses are offered in higher education, there should be no shortage of instructors familiar with some aspect of your scholarly interests.

- Talk to other students in the class. After all, they are familiar with the assignment and will probably be eager to bounce ideas off you as well.

- Explain the assignment to friends and family members. Perhaps they can suggest a particular angle on the topic that combines your interests with the assignment.

Getting Unstuck: Use E-Mail to Generate Ideas

E-mail is an excellent way to solicit input and advice. E-mail obviously allows you to contact a broader range of people, but the format has other advantages, as well:

- Some people find it easier to write down their questions than to communicate them face-to-face.
- While you might forget a suggestion you hear during a face-to-face exchange, in e-mail a response is recorded.

Exchange e-mail addresses with other students in your class. Sometimes class and work schedules make it difficult to meet to talk, but everybody reads his or her e-mail.

Getting Unstuck: Browse for Inspiration

Try browsing various information sources to stimulate your thinking. Below, we've provided a list of good places to start. Remember, though, many of the sources listed may not be suitable as research sources but will provide you with ideas about how best to approach your essay.

Encyclopedias Whether online or in print-format, encyclopedias are excellent resources for browsing for inspiration. Encyclopedias present general introductions to a wide range of topics and are well suited to skimming.

Print encyclopedias are available in virtually all types of libraries, including your school library and the local public library. While the most popular encyclopedias are comprehensive, there are many that focus on specific topics, such as art, nations (e.g., Canada), and medicine. The more popular general print encyclopedias include:

- *Encyclopedia Britannica*
- *Funk & Wagnalls*
- *Columbia Encyclopedia*

Web-based encyclopedias are increasingly popular. These offer the obvious advantages of easy and fast searching, but they also are well suited to identifying associations between related ideas—helping you stumble upon new information that you otherwise would have missed.

The largest general-interest online encyclopedia is *Wikipedia* (<www.wikipedia.org>) **(see Figure 1.1)**. However, *Wikipedia* is an open-source format, which means that contributions and modifications to the content are done by virtually anyone, regardless

FIGURE 1.1

Due to its relative high number of contributors, *Wikipedia* often includes information on subjects that other, traditional encyclopedias don't include, such as the above data on the Australian national cricket team.

of their knowledge level or agenda. Unlike traditional encyclopedias, *Wikipedia* is not reviewed by subject experts for accuracy or objectivity. While this allows *Wikipedia* to grow the volume of its entries quickly, and to be more up to date than most encyclopedias, it also means that it cannot serve as an authoritative source for academic research papers.

Other general-interest online encyclopedias include:

<http://encarta.msn.com>

<www.brittanica.com>

<www.encyclopedia.com>

<www.bartleby.com>

At this time, many of the online encyclopedias charge a fee for access to their information, often through an annual subscription. As well, some of them integrate advertising into their content and, at times, it's difficult to determine the difference between

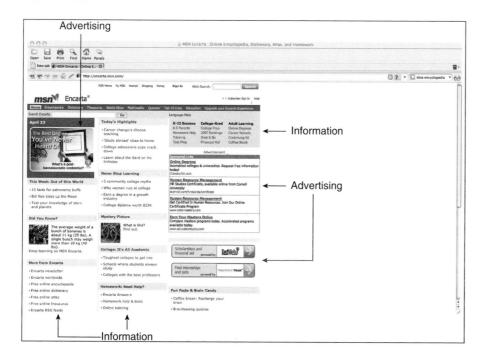

Advertising

Information

Advertising

Information

FIGURE 1.2

Microsoft Encarta was one of the first online encyclopedias. As is evident in this image, many of the advertisements on the page relate to the subject matter and are visually similar, making distinguishing among the types of information more difficult.

information and advertisements **(see Figure 1.2)**. If possible, access online encyclopedias through your college or university library to avoid paying fees and the distraction of advertisements. If you are not sure what encyclopedias are available through your library, ask a librarian for assistance.

Newspapers, Radio, and Television   A great source of topical and current issues is traditional media: newspapers, radio, and television. Many of the more popular sources provide their content resources online free of charge. If it is not free or available entirely on the web, then your university or local library system may have full-text versions available through paid subscriptions that usually can be accessed using your student identification information. (Ask your librarian for assistance, if required.) Below is a sample of some of the best from each category:

Newspapers:

- *The Globe and Mail* <www.globeandmail.com>
- *National Post* <www.canada.com/nationalpost>

- *Toronto Star* <www.thestar.com>
- *The Gazette* (Montreal) <www.canada.com/montrealgazette>
- *The Vancouver Sun* <www.canada.com/vancouversun>
- *The Chronicle Herald* (Halifax) <www.thechronicleherald.ca>
- *Winnipeg Free Press* <www.winnipegfreepress.com>
- *The Guardian* (UK) <www.guardian.co.uk>
- *The New York Times* <www.nytimes.com>
- *The Economist* (economics, politics, and business with European emphasis; **see Figure 1.3**) <www.economist.com>

It's important to remember that the vast majority of information available through popular media is not written by experts, but by journalists. Journalists are experts at quickly identifying and writing (or recording) compelling, bite-sized units of information that can

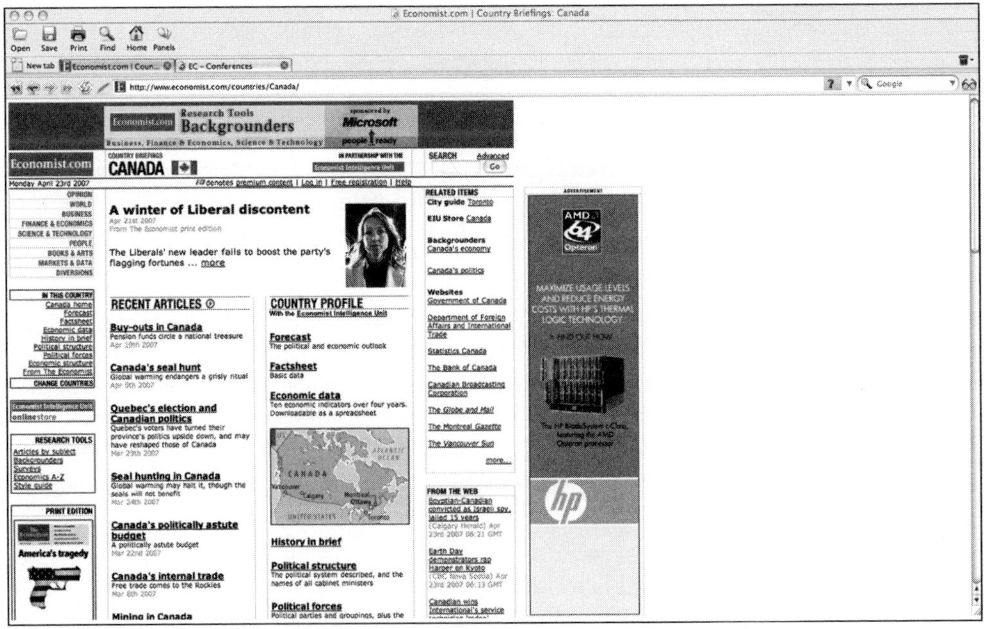

FIGURE 1.3

The Economist is distributed weekly and provides an excellent review of many of the key issues in global business and politics.

be consumed quickly by a wide range of audiences. You will eventually need to learn what experts (i.e., scholars or scientists) are saying through further research.

Radio:

- *NPR* <www.npr.org>
- *CBC* <www.cbc.ca>
- *BBC* <www.bbc.co.uk>

Television:

- *CBC* <www.cbc.ca>
- *CTV News Net* <www.ctv.ca>
- *CNN* <www.cnn.com>
- *PBS* <www.pbs.org> **(see Figure 1.4)**

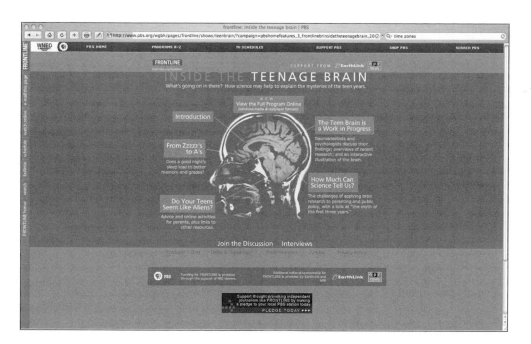

FIGURE 1.4

PBS, the U.S. public television network, operates one of the world's more useful education and news websites. Much of the information is organized by program.

Getting Stuck: What If I Still Can't Think of a Good Topic?

Search Engines   As discussed earlier, popular search engines like *Google* and *Yahoo!* are not usually the best starting point for in-depth scholarly research. But if you have tried everything else and are still casting about for an idea, popular search engines can help you determine a direction for your project. A simple keyword search will sometimes reveal interesting viewpoints and ideas.

All search engines are not created equal. Some search word for word through the entire text, some organize websites into categories, and some are directories that do not search the entire web. When browsing, your best choice would be a subject directory, such as:

- *Librarians' Internet Index* <www.lii.org>
- *InfoMine* <http://infomine.ucr.edu>
- *The Internet Public Library* <www.ipl.org>
- *The Virtual Library* <http://vlib.org>

QUICK CHECK

Discover a Topic

Discover a topic you want to know more about.

- Discuss the project with the course instructor, other instructors who teach in the subject area, other students, family, and/or friends.
- Browse encyclopedias, newspapers, and general search engines (*Yahoo!*, *Google*).
- Consider topics or issues you've encountered in other classes, and how they relate to your proposed research topic.

Refining Your Topic Selection

Once you have selected a topic for your research paper, your next step is to ensure that your research (1) asks a good question, and (2) is sufficiently focused.

Ask a Good Question

One of the most important skills in research is the ability to turn a general idea for a research topic into a clear and useful research question. It is a skill anyone can obtain; it simply takes practice. To get started, consider how some topics invite discussion or debate, while others simply recycle popular opinion (which may or may not be knowledgeable or informed). Consider, also, how good research questions focus on *how* and *why*, rather than on merely *what* or *where*.

Poor research question:	*Good research question:*
1. What TV shows contain violence?	**1.** Should television networks restrict violent programming in response to objections by religious and parental advocacy groups?
2. What e-commerce businesses have proven successful?	**2.** Why have certain e-commerce businesses been successful while others have failed?
3. Where are the best hospitals located?	**3.** How have the best hospitals in the country achieved their superior status?

Narrow Your Focus

Students very often make the mistake of keeping the topics of their research papers very broad and general. They do this because they fear that a narrow focus will mean they will quickly run out of things to say, and because narrowly focused research questions seem less "grand" and important to students than broader and more general questions. However, it is common for students to present their instructors with research papers on subjects better suited to an entire book than a short paper.

The best research papers begin with a carefully delineated and focused assertion that is then methodically substantiated by specific examples, evidence, and analysis. If you begin with a broad assertion, you will be hard-pressed to provide adequate (or interesting) support for all that you claim. When it comes to research papers, it is generally better to say a lot about a little rather than a little about a lot.

Too broad:

- Children should have rights in our society.

Focused:

- School locker searches are a violation of civil rights.
- Drug testing should be banned from high-school sports.

- Teen curfews are undemocratic.
- High-school newspapers should not be censored by school administration.

Remember three important questions when determining the scope of your research assignment.

1. What is the assigned length of the project?

If your instructor expects a 10-page essay, then your topic needs to be both focused and sufficiently complex. On the other hand, choose a less-involved subject—or just part of one—if the assignment is only 3 to 5 pages long; otherwise, you will merely scratch the surface of your topic. Superficial treatments are never effective in academic writing. For example, in 10 to 15 pages you could create a credible argument supporting the need for laws that require children to wear helmets when bicycling. If the assigned length is 3 pages, you might choose to narrow your subject to a discussion of how helmets have proven to protect children involved in bicycling accidents.

2. How much time do you have available to complete the project?

Any well-executed research project is time consuming. However, certain topics require greater amounts of time. Be sure you have allowed enough time to complete the assignment. If, for example, your topic requires interviewing experts or conducting surveys and compiling results, you need to allow time for this. Regardless of the type of research you are doing, make sure you limit your topic so you will have enough time to gather the necessary information. For instance, you might be interested in investigating the effectiveness of stalking laws. You could make this subject more manageable by limiting your discussion to the success rate of such laws in your own province or municipality.

3. Do I have the necessary resources to complete the research project?

The Internet has made it possible to obtain a great deal of information that was formerly inaccessible or highly inconvenient to obtain. Nevertheless, information on certain topics may be too difficult for you to access given the resources and time you have available. Moreover, certain research topics are so new or obscure that very little has been written on the subject. In these situations, you may not be able to find enough information to support a research paper.

Quality research requires that you develop a thorough understanding of the topic. Therefore, if after extensive investigation you discover there is insufficient information on the subject, you must either reject the topic or refocus it in a more promising direction. If, on the other hand, you discover an overwhelming amount of information on the subject, you must be careful to correctly identify the most relevant information, without misrepresenting or oversimplifying the subject.

Once you have chosen a topic and narrowed your focus, you are ready to begin to explore the different types of sources available (e.g., books, periodicals, websites, interviews, surveys). As your familiarity with these various resources develops, you may find that you develop an individualized approach to this process—methods and tactics that work especially well for you. However, certain time-tested strategies will remain constant. These research strategies are discussed in later chapters.

Example

- ***When a research topic is too new!***

  In the year 2000, MP3s (digital audio files that can be distributed over the Internet) were just beginning to surface, and little information existed about them beyond explanations of what they are and how they operate. A researcher would have been frustrated by the quantity and quality of the information available. However, because of the threat the downloading of MP3s poses to the multimillion-dollar recording industry, there has been a great deal of discussion about the commercial impact and ethical concerns surrounding this phenomenon during the past decade. Today, a student who chose this topic would find numerous sources with far-ranging opinions (**see Figure 1.5**).

QUICK CHECK

Determine Project Scope
- The BEST topics are specific and focused.
- Restrict your project to a topic or task you can complete successfully.
- Determine the scope of your topic to meet
    - » the assigned length of the project
    - » the time you have to complete the project
    - » the resources you have at your disposal

FIGURE 1.5

A search in this database revealed 3,363 periodical articles on MP3s. Prior to 1999 (when MP3s were first marketed), there was very little written about these recordings.

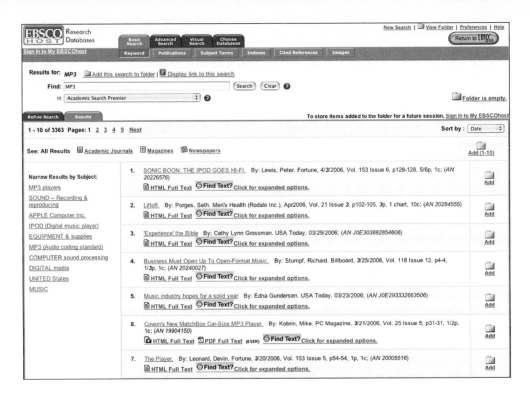

EXERCISES

1. People write best when they write about topics they consider interesting. But to choose a relevant topic, you must know yourself. To help you understand your interests, complete the following phrases as honestly and completely as you can.

   • The subject I most enjoy reading about is . . .

   • My favourite hobby or pastime is . . .

   • If I won the lottery, I would use the money to . . .

   • The type of volunteer activity I prefer is . . .

- My favourite school subject has always been . . .
- If I ran the world, the first thing I would change would be . . .

2. Make a list of four or five things that tick you off. (Choose significant things that others might experience, as well. For instance, your little brother or your mother-in-law might tick you off, but there is little chance that this annoyance will yield a possible paper topic.) Meet in a small group (four or five) of other classmates and share your lists. Brainstorm together about how to transform these frustrations into viable research topics.

3. Your biology professor has assigned a research paper on "biological warfare." To get an overview of this topic and to begin to determine the specific focus for your project, access an online encyclopedia to locate as much current information as possible. As you browse these resources, keep in mind the interests you identified in Exercise 1 and list two potential topics or research questions that combine your personal interests with the issue of biological warfare.

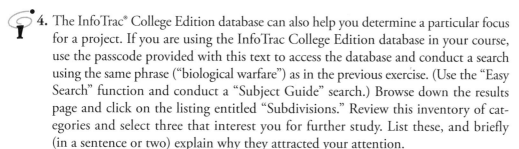

4. The InfoTrac® College Edition database can also help you determine a particular focus for a project. If you are using the InfoTrac College Edition database in your course, use the passcode provided with this text to access the database and conduct a search using the same phrase ("biological warfare") as in the previous exercise. (Use the "Easy Search" function and conduct a "Subject Guide" search.) Browse down the results page and click on the listing entitled "Subdivisions." Review this inventory of categories and select three that interest you for further study. List these, and briefly (in a sentence or two) explain why they attracted your attention.

5. Return to the same "results" list from your InfoTrac College Edition database search on "biological warfare" in Exercise 4 and click on "Related Subjects" (this appears just below the "Subdivisions" link). Choose ONE of these related subjects (the one that seems most intriguing to you) and then click on the "Subdivisions" link for this topic. Write a paragraph that explains why you chose this particular "Related Subject" (stipulate what made it more interesting to you than the others). Also indicate which ONE of the subdivisions under this subject seems most interesting to you and why.

2 Finding Good Information

"What is research, but a blind date with knowledge?"

WILLIAM HENRY

Once you have successfully chosen a topic for your project, the next step is to locate the information you need to answer your research questions and present a convincing analysis or argument. This chapter provides you with a roadmap to find the best information in the quickest way possible.

Internet vs. Library Search

Before the Internet became a common tool in colleges and universities, students were typically limited to the resources available in their school and public libraries or through interlibrary loans. Consequently, students had access to far fewer resources to use in research papers. The Internet has dramatically increased the volume of information available, and made it easier and faster to find that information. With the click of a mouse, you can connect and communicate with countless potential sources for your investigation.

Three Common Problems with Using the Internet for Academic Research

The Internet has also created new potential problems for the novice researcher. Begin by reviewing these problems so you can be sure to avoid them.

1. Too Many Hits

The most common complaint students have about doing research on the web is the sheer number of hits they get when conducting a keyword search. A search for a specific subject or item can turn up hundreds, or even thousands, of results **(see Figure 2.1)**. Sifting through

FIGURE 2.1

A simple Internet search
using the keyword "bicycle
helmets" resulted in 2,090,000
matches.

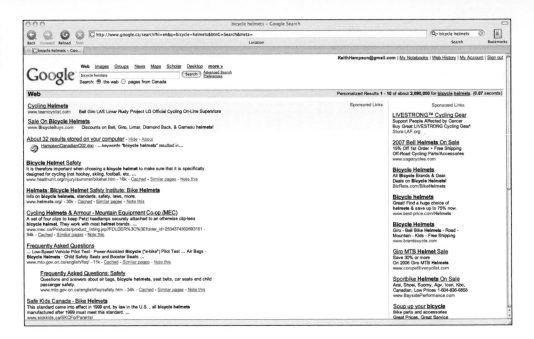

all of these results to evaluate their relevance for your particular project is a time-consuming and overwhelming task. Although search engines are great for obtaining certain types of information (e.g., which camera is best suited to your photography needs), much of the research you will be required to do during your academic career might be too complex and nuanced for a simple search using *Google, Yahoo!,* or other popular search engines.

2. Irrelevant Hits

Another related problem is that your search will probably return numerous sites that are totally unrelated to your topic. This often occurs because search engines use criteria for identifying web pages that are different than your research criteria. For example, many search engines—including the now-ubiquitous *Google*—use the popularity of the web page to determine its value for each new search. (Specifically, *Google* ranks each website by the number of times other websites link to it.) Thus, the more popular the website, the higher

FIGURE 2.2

The results of this web search for "online dating" using *Google* included very few academic studies of the subject.

it will rank in search results (i.e., it will be one of the first hits). But the popularity of a web page is not always a reflection of its value, particularly for academic research **(see Figure 2.2)**. It's entirely possible that the most useful web pages (accurate, intelligent, credible) are also the least popular.

3. Non-Credible Information

While the previous problems may make your Internet searches frustrating and time consuming, perhaps nothing undermines the legitimacy of an academic research project more than unreliable websites. The Internet has dramatically increased our access to information, but it has also dramatically increased the ease with which anyone can publish information. For the first time in history, it is now possible for anyone (with rudimentary computer skills) to publish information accessible to a vast audience.

In the pre-Internet days, students collected the bulk of their information from school or public libraries; this may have limited the volume of information available, but the student could be largely assured that these resources were reliable because editors in publishing companies, subject-matter experts, and librarians had already evaluated them and found them legitimate. However, no such methods of control determine what's published on many, if not most, websites. Thus, a student must evaluate each web page to determine whether the information is accurate and reliable. This is not always easy to discern, and it makes any research done on the web particularly challenging. A strong thesis must, after all, be based on reliable information.

Library Search Strategies

While simply typing in a few keywords on *Google* may seem the easiest way toward finding the information you need, it isn't. **Library collections are the best starting point for conducting academic research.** The results of your research within a library will generate more credible and relevant results for the simple reason that these libraries are designed to serve the needs of people—like you—doing academic research **(see Figure 2.3)**. And, because libraries are now adopting many of the search technologies that services like *Google* have advanced, your research within the library system will be convenient and easy.

Library Resources: Online and On-Site

Some online reference catálogues can be accessed only from computer terminals located in the school's library, but most colleges and universities have connected their catalogues to the web, making it possible for students to conduct research remotely. You still have to visit the library to check out books and access many of the holdings, but for numerous activities you are no longer restricted to the hours your library is open.

Internet technology has made it possible for even the smallest school libraries to offer impressive collections, and it has made it easier, once you know how the systems work, to access them.

Please note that college and university libraries often charge fees for printing research materials from school computers. Printing bibliographies of potential resources or full-text articles can be expensive. However, many online systems allow you to e-mail your search findings (which you can then print at your home computer). You may want to do the bulk of your searching from a computer with free or relatively inexpensive printing.

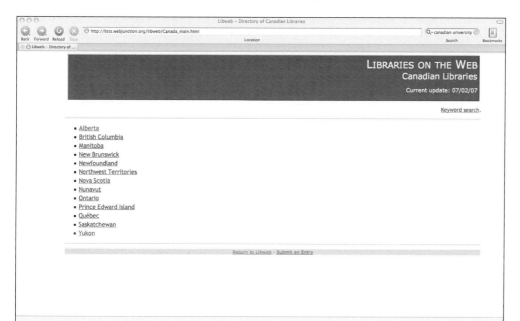

FIGURE 2.3

This website offers links to thousands of online catalogues, including Canadian colleges and universities, public libraries, and international libraries.

Interlibrary Loan The Internet has made interlibrary loans easier and quicker. Some schools even allow you to order interlibrary loans online. Interlibrary loans from these schools often take less than a week to complete. Also, check to see if your school has agreements with other colleges or universities to share library resources. In many areas of Canada, colleges and universities have linked their online catalogues so that students can search just their own or all of the libraries for materials. You may even be able to visit and use other school libraries in your area if the schools have an agreement. Check with your library for details.

Types of Library Resources You might already have a preference for the types of materials you like to use (probably because you have experienced success with one type when doing a research project in the past), but don't limit yourself. *Explore.* Expand your knowledge of what's available to you. To do that, you need to understand what types of resources are available to you.

General and Special Reference Works   Every library has a reference section. It is usually located in an especially accessible area, often near the front of the library, and reference librarians who can assist you staff it. Materials in this section cannot normally be checked out, and typically include:

- encyclopedias
- dictionaries
- atlases
- almanacs
- biographical references

Reference sections also include special reference works, including not only general encyclopedias and dictionaries but also materials devoted to specific disciplines.

At some point early in your studies, browse the reference section to get a sense of the resources available, especially those specific to your major and related areas of interest. Some of these reference works (like general encyclopedias and dictionaries) are now available online (see the discussion in Chapter 1 about online encyclopedias and newspapers), but many special reference works are available only at the library. Some of the special reference works that might be housed in the general reference section include:

- *Business and the Environment: A Resource Guide*
- *The Bulfinch Guide to Art History: A Comprehensive Survey and Dictionary of Western Art and Architecture*
- *FP Markets: Canadian Demographics*
- *Dictionary of Mathematics*

Because its resources will provide general overviews of your topic, the reference section can be an excellent starting point for your research. However, because the information contained in these works is so general, you ultimately will need to extend your search beyond them.

Books   When you hear the word "library," books probably leap to mind. Library books are housed in the "stacks" (the main bookcases of the library), arranged according to subject categories determined by the Library of Congress, and can be checked out and removed from the library. Sometimes one author writes them; sometimes they contain collections of essays or chapters written by many experts—not all who necessarily share the same point of view or perspective.

TIP

The Library of Congress Classification (LCC) is a system used in many parts of the world for organizing library collections.

Periodicals   Periodicals are publications like newspapers, magazines, and scholarly journals that are issued at regular intervals (e.g., daily, weekly, monthly). You might be familiar with periodicals like *The Globe and Mail, Maclean's,* and *The Economist,* but you may be less familiar with the many scholarly periodicals available in your library. The articles in these journals are written by experts in their fields, typically academics, rather than reporters or journalists. As well, periodicals are published more quickly and therefore are more up to date. Periodicals, because they frequently are published on more perishable materials, are also the most "polymorphous" holdings in the library—you may find them available in their original "hard" (or printed on paper) state, on microfiche, on microfilm, or, increasingly, in computer databases. Many of the most recently created periodical publications exist exclusively online.

Libraries: Online Resources

Library research used to require hours spent shuffling through stacks of index cards in drawer after drawer of the card catalogue—and taking note of potentially promising call numbers. However, computers have made the card catalogue a thing of the past, and almost all library reference systems are now electronic. Learning to use your school's online catalogue has a number of benefits that go beyond the obvious one of locating books, journal articles, or other resources available through your library system. It offers the perfect starting point for learning to effectively use electronic search tools.

Smaller libraries often have limited print-based periodical resources. However, a new breed of databases (e.g., WilsonSelect, SIRSResearcher, Academic Search Elite [EBSCOhost], InfoTrac College Edition [Gale]) offers full-text periodical articles. How to use these databases will be discussed more fully in future chapters.

Searching Library Systems

Although computer search tools may differ slightly in appearance and in the features they offer, they all operate similarly. Whether you are using an Internet search engine, a database, or an online reference catalogue, you simply type in a keyword or phrase that identifies

FIGURE 2.4

This online reference catalogue allows you to search by keyword, author, title, or subject. The search screen for your library's catalogue might appear slightly different from this, but most operate very similarly.

Image published with permission of ProQuest LLC. Further reproduction is prohibited without permission.

your subject, click on a "begin search" button, and then wait for the computer to list all of the documents that match your request.

When you are using an online reference catalogue search tool, you can search according to a keyword, an author's name, the title of a work, or a subject category. Some search tools offer other options as well, but these are the main categories for which you will usually search (**see Figure 2.4**). At the beginning of a research project, you will primarily use the **keyword** or **subject** option.

The Difference Between Keyword and Subject Searches   It is important to understand the difference between keyword and subject searches. A **keyword search** retrieves all documents that include the specified word(s), whether the words appear in the subject headings, title, or description of the article or book. In an online database or Internet search engine, a keyword search might search the entire text of the document. A **subject search**, on the other hand, retrieves documents that have been catalogued under that particular subject

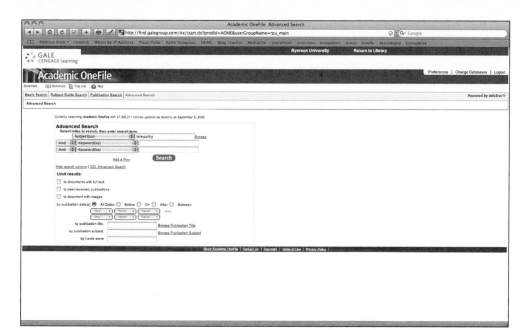

FIGURE 2.5

Many databases, like Academic OneFile, include "pull-down" menus that allow you to select among subject, keyword, author, and other search criteria.

heading. In an online catalogue and some databases, such headings are determined by the Library of Congress Classification system. There are advantages and drawbacks to both types of searches.

Understanding the differences between keyword and subject searches will enable you to conduct the most effective searches **(see Figure 2.5)**.

Keyword Search

- Any words that *could* be used to describe your topic *can* be used (extremely flexible and broad)

- Most useful at the beginning of a project when you don't know the exact language used by experts on your topic

- Search will fail completely if you don't locate or guess the correct keywords

Subject Search

- May retrieve many results that aren't relevant to your topic
- The *exact* terms that describe a topic as determined by the Library of Congress or subject index must be used
- Definitely the most effective type of search if you know the exact terms because it retrieves only the most relevant documents

Accurate Term Selection   While the operation seems very simple, if you have used a search tool you know that success or failure depends on your ability to match your search terms with the documents you are trying to retrieve **(see Figure 2.6)**. Even simple spelling errors can block your efforts. A student in one of my classes once spent a very frustrating 40 minutes in the online reference catalogue and then brusquely informed me that our library contained absolutely nothing about Albert Einstein. I was a bit mystified until

FIGURE 2.6

A basic search within a library database produced six mostly relevant results.

I looked at his computer screen and saw that he had been using the search term "Albert Einstine." When he corrected his error, he, of course, had a wide range of documents to choose from. Even if you spell correctly, the most effective search terms may not be the ones that immediately come to mind.

Electronic search tools seek precise matches to your search terms or phrases. Besides spelling mistakes, another common error students sometimes make is capitalizing words that are not proper nouns. Remember that some search engines are *case sensitive;* capitalize only when appropriate.

TIP

Keep a running list of possible search terms and phrases as you try, by trial and error, to find keywords that match your topic. A keyword that was unsuccessful in the online catalogue might work in a database or Internet search engine. It takes very little time to jot down a word or phrase, and it could save you much time and effort later. There are a number of ways you can expand your list of keywords.

The problem with electronic search tools is that although they are much quicker, and usually more thorough, than humans, they can't think. That is your job. However, this is not to say that you are confined to your own (perhaps, at least initially, limited) understanding of your topic. Numerous support systems are available to help you assemble a list of possible search words and phrases.

Identify Synonyms or Related Words or Ideas You might have chosen a topic for which you can readily identify keywords. For example, if you have chosen to research reasons why marijuana should be legalized for medical purposes, the key terms "marijuana," "legalization," and "medicine" almost leap out at you. Even in this fairly straightforward example, however, there are certain pitfalls you need to be familiar with. For instance, marijuana can also be spelled *marihuana.*

However, not all topics translate so quickly into search terms that will result in finding the information you need. If, for instance, you chose to investigate how communities regulate dog and cat populations, you might try the term "animal control." While this might seem like the obvious term (after all, agencies responsible for catching stray dogs and cats are often called "animal control" by local governments), a search using this phrase

Economics of Higher Education

Key terms
1. *"higher education"*
2. *"cost of higher education"*
3. *"rising tuition"*
4. *"university" and "cost"*
5.
6.
7.

turned up documents that dealt with livestock, laboratory animals, and wild animals, but nothing about controlling stray or homeless pets.

You have two choices at this point. On the one hand, you could (like my student who informed me that he couldn't locate anything about Albert Einstein) assume that your library has no information on your topic. The better solution is to discover alternative words or phrases that relate to your subject. For instance, stray cats and dogs are frequently held in "animal shelters," and in some areas of the country these shelters are run by "humane societies."

Sometimes a dictionary or thesaurus can help you locate a successful keyword. One of my students wanted to examine how colleges and universities are responding to the special problems of foreign students who choose to study in Canada. Searches using the phrase "foreign students" resulted in no matches. After consulting a thesaurus for synonyms, she experienced success with the phrase "international students."

Use a Thesaurus   Word-processing programs typically include a thesaurus. Computer versions of thesauri have shorter lists of optional words than their hard-copy counterparts, but they are much easier to use. Also, scanning alternative words for the synonyms in the original list can lead you to additional lists of possible keywords. You can also use the *Merriam-Webster Online Thesaurus* at <www.m-w.com>.

Refer to the Library of Congress Classification System   Since all materials in the library are organized according to standardized categories (unlike the Internet, which is a space in which documents might be organized under any number of terms or phrases), the Library of Congress classification system can help you discover the key terms and phrases used by academics to describe your topic and match you up with the best resources available. You will find the *Library of Congress Subject Headings* (a four-volume work) in the reference section of your library or online at <www.loc.gov/catdir/cpso/lcco>. It can help you discover optional terms for your topic that you might not have thought of on your own.

Suppose you are investigating the way fashion reflects contemporary culture's preoccupation with technology. Looking up "fashion" in the *Library of Congress Subject Headings* would lead you to the terms "Manners and Customs" (the general heading) and "Costume," "Dress," "Materials and articles of clothing," and "Ornaments"—alternatives that might be more successful because they are more narrowly focused on your topic. Part of investigating a new subject is learning the language used by those who are experts in that field. Use the well-established subject categories of your library to help you identify the words that will call up the best information when you search **(see Figure 2.7)**.

Library of Congress Classifications   Your reference librarian can direct you to a list of Library of Congress subject categories, but you can also view these online. See *LC Classification Outline* at <www.loc.gov>.

Construct Boolean Search Phrases   I still remember the first time I was asked to conduct a *Boolean search*. The name alone seemed both ridiculous and intimidating. When the librarian (by way of explanation) distributed four or five handouts filled with confusing Venn diagrams, I was sure I would never understand. I've always been a bit math impaired, and Venn diagrams sounded and looked suspiciously similar to something I might have encountered in a statistics or calculus class. Imagine my surprise when I realized that the idea is not only very simple but also very useful. In fact, if you do much surfing on the web, whether you know it or not you have probably already done a Boolean search.

FIGURE 2.7

The subject categories listed in the *LC Classification Outline* suggest narrowly focused terms under more general topics.

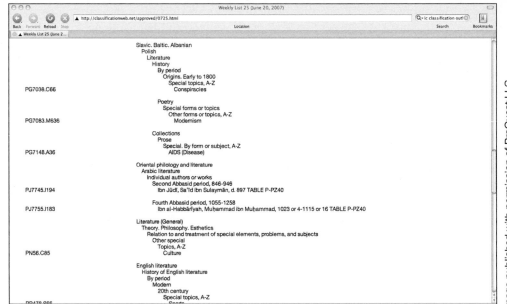

Image published with permission of ProQuest LLC.
Further reproduction is prohibited without permission.

I became less frightened when I realized that the system's odd-sounding name was merely the result of having been created by George Boole. Even though Boole was a mathematician (thus the Venn diagrams), you don't have to be a rocket scientist to understand the process. A Boolean search refines your quest by linking keywords with **AND, OR,** or **NOT** to demonstrate the relationships between the terms. Most research projects have a narrow focus, and Boolean phrases allow you to pinpoint the types of documents that directly address your topic.

A few years ago a student who worked in a pet store decided to investigate the law that forbids the sale of turtles less than four inches in size. The law was enacted to protect consumers from the threat of salmonella poisoning. Her argument was that the law, although well meaning, was illogical. Salmonella can be spread by any number of reptiles (not just turtles), and infection is not limited to small turtles. After compiling a simple list of keywords ("turtles," "reptiles," "salmonella"), she organized them into search phrases using the Boolean term **AND** (Boolean terms are always capitalized to distinguish them from the

0134112543610

QUICK CHECK

A Brief Guide to Boolean Logic

Boolean **AND** *requires all terms to be in records retrieved.*

   Example: *turtles AND salmonella*

Boolean **OR** *allows either term.*

   Example: *turtles OR reptiles*

Boolean **NOT** *excludes terms.*

   Example: *salmonella NOT "food poisoning"*

Combine terms using parentheses (actions in parentheses will be performed first).

   Example: *(turtle OR reptile) AND (salmonella NOT "food poisoning")*

Enclose multiword search phrases in quotation marks.

   Example: *"food poisoning"*

keywords), indicating that both terms in the following examples should appear in the search results.

- turtles **AND** salmonella

- reptiles **AND** salmonella

However, when my student attempted to use these Boolean phrases in her school's online catalogue, there were no matches. While these terms are clearly connected to the topic (and may prove productive in another search engine), they did not trigger the desired response in the online library catalogue. Therefore, this researcher had to rethink her list of keywords. Her first strategy was to abandon the Boolean terms and conduct a simple keyword search using just the term "turtle."

However, this proved unfruitful **(see Figure 2.8)**. The solution to this problem is not to think more generally but to determine how the information you are looking for specifically differs from what you are finding.

A quick look at the results of the "turtle" keyword search reveals documents about sea turtles, fictional turtles, Ninja turtles, and by publishers with the word "turtle" in their name. When I asked this student how these "turtles" differed from what she was searching for, she readily answered that she was searching for "pet" turtles. She conducted two new

Casa Loma Library
George Brown College

FIGURE 2.8

A search using the term "turtle" produces 916 hits, and most appear totally unrelated to the topic.

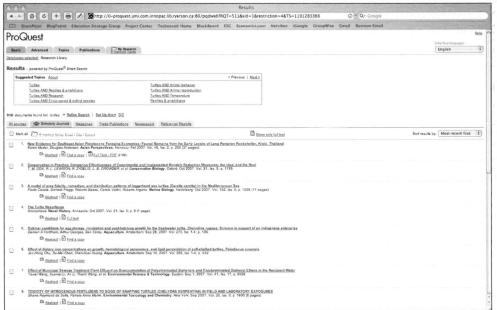

Image published with permission of ProQuest LLC.
Further reproduction is prohibited without permission.

Boolean searches:

- turtles **AND** pets
- reptiles **AND** pets

These searches returned documents that were more appropriate **(see Figure 2.9)**.

Combining phrases is a way to *refine* your search. By this I mean that a Boolean search weeds out unrelated documents and produces matches that directly address your topic. The two preceding searches could be combined into one by using the Boolean term **OR** (use parentheses to group search phrases).

(turtles **OR** reptiles) **AND** pets

My student soon determined that she needed to learn more about salmonella (how it is transmitted, the symptoms, treatment, etc.). She conducted a simple search using the keyword "salmonella" and soon discovered that food poisoning, as well as reptiles, can cause

Image published with permission of ProQuest LLC.
Further reproduction is prohibited without permission.

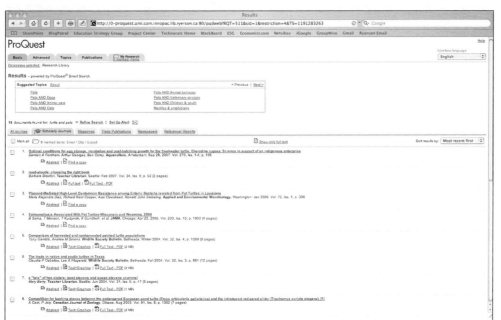

FIGURE 2.9

The results of the search for "pets AND turtles" include only 18 documents, and many appear to be directly related to the researcher's topic.

salmonella. Therefore, she refined her search by excluding the terms "food poisoning" (multiword search terms should be enclosed in quotation marks) with the Boolean term **NOT:**

> salmonella **NOT** "food poisoning"

Electronic search tools vary. Some allow you to use complicated search phrases; others can't respond to more than one or two Boolean terms per search. It would be ideal if you could conduct a search such as the following:

> (turtles **OR** reptiles) **AND** (salmonella **NOT** "food poisoning")

Sometimes online search tools allow you to do such advanced searches (**see Figure 2.10**). It will take a certain amount of trial and error to determine what works best in your library's system.

FIGURE 2.10

This online catalogue offers a complex search that allows you to refine your query using up to a variety of different Boolean terms.

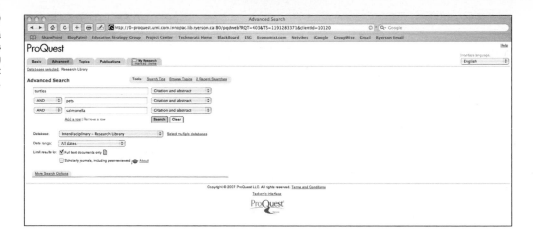

Boolean searches are simple if you remember four basic rules:

1. Use the Boolean terms **AND, OR,** or **NOT** to specify the relationships between keywords:
   - Use AND when you want both keywords to appear in the document: **turtles AND pets.** [Note: Some search tools require a plus sign (+) instead (e.g., turtles + pets).]
   - Use OR when either keyword can appear in the document: **turtles OR reptiles.**
   - Use NOT to exclude unwanted terms: **salmonella NOT "food poisoning."** [Note: Some search tools require a minus sign (−) instead (e.g., salmonella – "food poisoning").]

2. Always capitalize Boolean search terms **(AND, OR, NOT).**

3. Enclose groups of search terms in parentheses to indicate which actions should occur first: **(turtles OR reptiles) AND salmonella.**

4. Enclose multiword search terms in quotation marks: **salmonella NOT "food poisoning."**

It may not be as exciting as finding that perfect someone, but you will probably feel a certain satisfaction when your keyword and Boolean searches turn up sources that contain just the information you need to get started on a well-documented research essay.

As gratifying as this can be, it is only the starting point. The next chapter will discuss how to use your library's resources to continue to expand your search terms and refine your searches, connect with an even greater variety of sources, and evaluate which resources are best for your project.

QUICK CHECK

Identifying Keywords

Identify keywords that match your topic.

- Locate synonyms and alternative phrases for your topic.
- Discover the Library of Congress subject headings that address your topic.
- Combine your search terms into effective Boolean search phrases

Keep a running list of all search terms and phrases because different keywords will be successful in different research tools.

EXERCISES

1. Refer to the viable research topics you generated from the list of things that "tick you off" (Exercise 2 in Chapter 1). Work with a partner or a group of students to create a list of synonyms or alternative phrases for these topics.

2. The following topics frequently are the subject of student papers. For each of them, write as many synonyms or alternative phrases as you can discover.

   - School violence
   - Teen pregnancy
   - Domestic abuse
   - Antismoking laws
   - Narcotic laws

3. Using either the *Library of Congress Subject Headings* in your school library's reference section or an online guide (such as <http://lcweb.loc.gov/catdir/cpso/lcco/lcco.html>),

locate all of the Library of Congress (LC) subject headings that are pertinent to ONE of the topics listed in Exercise 2.

Enter your school's online catalogue and use these subject headings as subject search phrases to locate and list four sources that directly address the topic.

Print out the complete bibliographic information for these sources.

4. If you are using the InfoTrac College Edition database in your course, use the passcode provided with this textbook to access the database and conduct first a "Subject guide" search and then a "Keyword" search (click on the appropriate term in the menu on the left) for ONE of the topics listed in Exercise 2 (remember to enclose a multiword search term in quotation marks). Write a paragraph in which you describe the differences between the two search results and explain why these differences occur.

5. Combine the LC subject headings you identified in Exercise 3 with the synonyms and alternative phrases you discovered for that topic in Exercise 2 to create as many variant Boolean search phrases as you can (refer to the *Quick Check* on page 35 for help). Use the InfoTrac College Edition database and experiment with these search phrases to locate four sources that directly address the topic. (*Note:* Databases do not rely on LC subject headings in topic searches. Nevertheless, identifying the LC headings can help you refine your search.) Print out the complete bibliographic information for these sources.

3 Intelligent Search Strategies

"Research is the act of going up alleys to see if they are blind."

PLUTARCH

As Plutarch so aptly noted, the search for relevant information requires a willingness to explore paths that may ultimately lead nowhere. But, of course, we want to spend little time during our research going up blind alleys; we want to zero in on the best resources that support our research agenda. This chapter focuses on strategies that do just that.

Intelligent research strategies involve four key tactics:

- Transform your research topic into a series of research questions.
- Use research questions to identify new keywords and search phrases.
- Use promising research results to find other resources.
- Ensure the quality of your research sources.

Transform Your Research Topic into a Series of Research Questions

A good way to begin your research is by transforming your topic or thesis from a statement or assertion into a series of questions. To help you gain this focus, start by asking yourself, "What do I need to know to prove my point?"

For example, suppose (like Scott, one of my former students) you are interested in examining the ways provincial financial aid programs favour traditional students over nontraditional students. Scott had left a job with a good salary to return to school; however, he was shocked to discover that his previous income made him ineligible for financial aid (even though, as a full-time student, he was no longer employed). His experience led him to suspect that the financial aid system gives preference to students who are entering post-secondary education directly from high school. From this information, we can create our thesis statement.

FIGURE 3.1

A search of this online catalogue using the keywords "student aid" returned 4,095 potential sources.

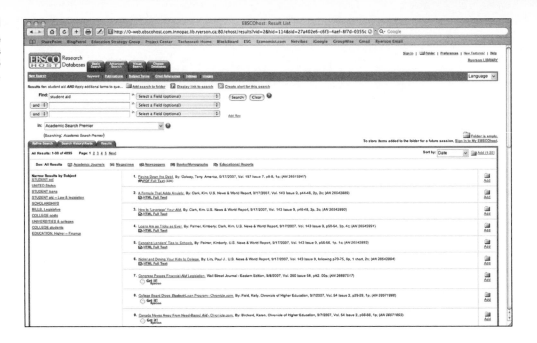

Thesis Statement: The current financial aid system gives preference to students entering college/university directly from high school.

But how could he be sure? His first attempts at searching in the online catalogue produced an overwhelming number of prospective sources **(see Figure 3.1)**.

At this point, Scott realized he needed to determine more exactly what information he needed to support his theory. Therefore, he composed a list of research questions that stem from his thesis statement.

Research Questions:

What are the criteria for student financial aid used by banks and governments?

Why do these criteria exist?

What is a "traditional" student in the eyes of the lenders?

What is a "nontraditional" student in the eyes of the lenders?

In what ways do the financial needs of traditional and nontraditional students differ?

What assumptions do colleges, universities, and financial aid agencies make about nontraditional students' needs?

Although he might have been able to give tentative answers to many of these questions before conducting any research, in order to construct a persuasive argument Scott knew he needed to locate sources that would give him up-to-date information generated by people who had facts to back up their claims. Identifying the specific facts, statistics, definitions, and ideas he was looking for enabled him to sift through the long list of potential sources more selectively. Rephrasing his thesis into a series of questions meant that he found the best resources available relatively quickly. He was able to recognize whether the sources he found were trustworthy and whether they provided information relevant to his project.

Use Research Questions to Identify New Keywords and Search Phrases

Scott was on the right track. However, he soon discovered that an even more effective method of research was to use these research questions to identify the keywords and Boolean phrases that would quickly reduce the number of documents the catalogue returned. Scott's first search used the keyword phrase "student aid," which produced 4,095 hits—too many to sift through! His research questions, however, suggested that he was most interested in a more specific issue: the distribution of financial aid for a particular kind of student. He first tried a Boolean search with the terms "student aid AND nontraditional student," but this did not match any of the library subject categories **(see Figure 3.2)**. (If you are unfamiliar with Boolean searches, see Chapter 2.)

Undaunted, Scott tried to think of synonyms for the type of student he considered "nontraditional." His subsequent search using the Boolean phrase "student aid AND adult" produced the results he sought **(see Figure 3.3)**.

As Scott's experience suggests, carefully composed questions and search terms will help you sift through extraneous information and locate the materials that address your subject directly. Like any good detective, the best researchers and writers are willing to change their minds if

FIGURE 3.2

The student attempted a
second search using "student
aid AND nontraditional
student." However, this
search uncovered
only one result.

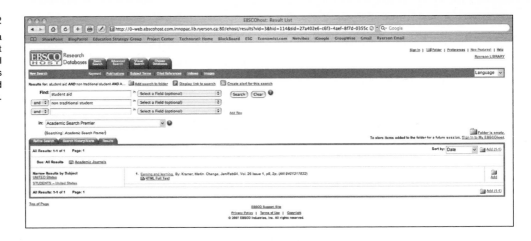

FIGURE 3.3

Refining a Boolean search so
that it calls for a specific type
of information (based on the
student's research questions)
produced a good selection of
mostly relevant hits.

confronted with new information. Keep in mind, too, that as you work on the project, your strategies might shift or change as you discover new questions that you need to answer in order to address your subject more fully or successfully. You may even find that the evidence requires modifying your initial thesis. Still, if you don't maintain a clear sense of focus, you will probably feel overwhelmed when you begin to explore online library or Internet resources.

Use Promising Research to Find Other Resources

It is very common in academic research for one "good find" to lead other good finds. When your research efforts uncover great source of information, this new source of information often will itself be the source of further excellent sources of information. A book, for example, might contain an excellent bibliography that yields five or six additional good sources. Similarly, a periodical article might reference another source that proves even more fruitful than the original.

Because one research source often leads to additional valuable sources, search tools in libraries are often set up to make following these leads intuitive. Online catalogues in libraries are designed expressly to help you track down promising leads **(see Figure 3.4)**.

TIP

» **Keep Track of Your Keywords**

Hyperlinks make it possible to move very quickly through many different keyword and subject category searches. When you find a promising new key term, add it to your list. You might find a search phrase will be successful in a subsequent database or Internet search. Also copy or print out information about any texts that seem appropriate to your search. There is nothing more frustrating than having to go back and spend additional time relocating a source that you spotted in a prior search.

Consider the example of the student who was interested in turtles and salmonella. Her most productive search phrase was "reptiles AND pets," which returned 22 titles. A quick glance at this list reveals one that seems particularly appropriate: *The Care of Reptiles and Amphibians in Captivity* by Chris Mattison. A click on that title brings up the full-display description that includes a list of subject categories under which this book has been catalogued **(see Figure 3.5)**. Two of the subject headings (the ones including the word "amphibian")

This book search uncovered a description of a book, as well as links to related information such as other publications by one of the authors.

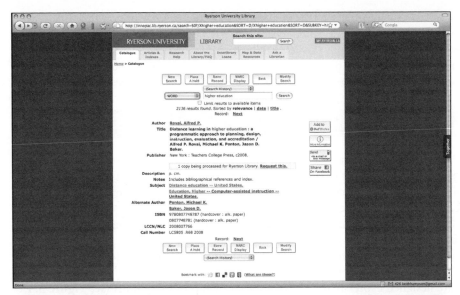

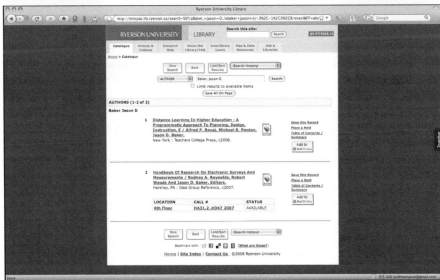

Format Book
Description 317 p., [16] p. of plates : ill. (some col.) ; 22 cm.

    Notes Includes bibliographical references (p. 303-306) and indexes.
  Contents General **care** -- Some biological considerations -- Thermoregulation; social
    behaviour -- Obtaining specimens and making a start -- Selecting species; legal
    aspects; selecting specimens; preparations -- Accommodation -- Cages; equipment --
    Creating **the** right environment -- Temperature control; lighting control; humidity
    control; control of biological factors; **the** planted vivarium -- Foods and feeding --
    Vegetable food; animal food; supplements; methods of feeding; water; overfeeding --
    Breeding -- Sex determination; conditioning; stimuli; mating; pregnancy; parturition;
    egg-laying; incubation; rearing young; breeding programmes -- Diseases --
    Controlling diseases; environmental diseases; nutritional diseases; bacterial infections;
    protozoan infections; endoparasites; ectoparasites; fungal infections; miscellaneous
    disorders -- Handling -- Descriptions of species and their maintenance -- Caudata:
    newts and salamanders -- Ambystomidae: Mole salamanders -- Salamandridae --
    Plethodontidae: Woodland salamanders -- Anura: frogs and toads -- Pipidae:
    tongueless frogs.
    (cont) Discoglossidae: fire-bellied toads, painted frog and midwife toad --
    Pelobatidae: spadefoot toads -- Ranidae -- Raninae: true frogs -- Mantellinae --
    Dendrobatidae: poison arrow frogs -- Rhacophoridae -- Microhylidae -- Bufonidae:
    true toads -- Hylidae: tree-frogs -- Leptodactylidae -- Crocodilia: crocodiles and
    alligators -- Chelonia: turtles and tortoises -- Pelomedusidae -- Chelidae: side-necked
    turtles -- Chelydridae: mud, musk and snapping turtles -- Emydidae: freshwater
    turtles -- Testudinidae: land tortoises -- Trionychidae: soft-shelled turtles -- Squamata:
    sub-order lacertilia: lizards -- Gekkonidae: geckos -- Eublepharinae --
    Sphaerodactylinae -- Gekkoninae -- Xantusidae: night lizards -- Iguanidae: iguanas --
    Agamidae: agamas -- Chamaeleontidae: chameleons -- Scincidae: skinks --
    Cordylidae: zonures -- Gerrhosauridae: plated lizards -- Lacertidae -- Teiidae: tegus
    and whiptails -- Anguidae: slow-worms, glass lizards and alligator lizards --
    Varanidae: monitors -- Amphisbaenidae -- Squamata: sub-order serpentes: snakes --
    Typhlopidae and leptotyphlopidae: blind snakes.
    (cont) Boidae: boas and pythons -- Colubridae: typical snakes -- Venomous snakes --
    Colubridae -- Elapidae: cobras -- Viperidae: vipers -- Viperinae -- Crotalinae: pit
    vipers -- Laws pertaining to **the** keeping of **reptiles** and **amphibians** --
    Herpetological societies.
    ISBN 0713723386
  Subject Captive **reptiles**.
        Captive **amphibians**.
        Pets **Amphibians**
        Pets **Reptiles**

FIGURE 3.5

The subject hyperlinks reveal
other Library of Congress categories under which this book
is catalogued, providing easy
access to additional sources
that might contain pertinent
information.

FIGURE 3.6

There are seven titles listed under the subject category "Captive reptiles"; several of them did not appear under the previous search phrase "reptiles AND pets."

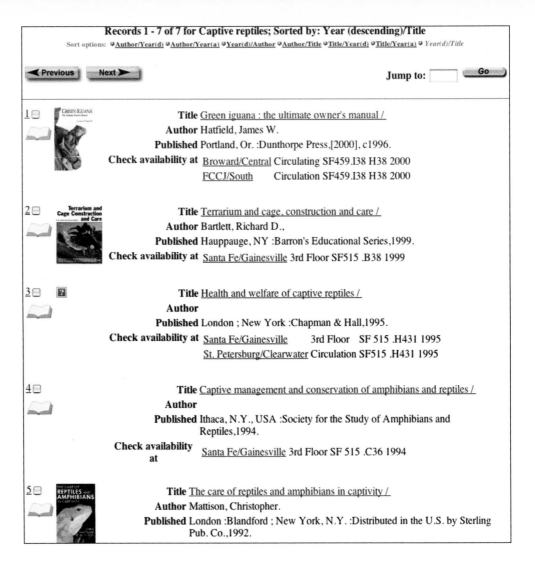

Records 1 - 7 of 7 for Captive reptiles; Sorted by: Year (descending)/Title

Sort options: ♦Author/Year(d) ♦Author/Year(a) ♦Year(d)/Author ♦Author/Title ♦Title/Year(d) ♦Title/Year(a) ♦ Year(d)/Title

◄ Previous   Next ►   Jump to: [   ]   Go

1 ☐   GREEN IGUANA   Title Green iguana : the ultimate owner's manual /
                      Author Hatfield, James W.
                      Published Portland, Or. :Dunthorpe Press,[2000], c1996.
        Check availability at Broward/Central Circulating SF459.I38 H38 2000
                               FCCJ/South   Circulation SF459.I38 H38 2000

2 ☐ Terrarium and   Title Terrarium and cage, construction and care /
     Cage Construction Author Bartlett, Richard D.,
        and Care   Published Hauppauge, NY :Barron's Educational Series,1999.
        Check availability at Santa Fe/Gainesville 3rd Floor SF515 .B38 1999

3 ☐   [?]   Title Health and welfare of captive reptiles /
                      Author
                      Published London ; New York :Chapman & Hall,1995.
        Check availability at Santa Fe/Gainesville   3rd Floor   SF 515 .H431 1995
                               St. Petersburg/Clearwater Circulation SF515 .H431 1995

4 ☐   Title Captive management and conservation of amphibians and reptiles /
                      Author
                      Published Ithaca, N.Y., USA :Society for the Study of Amphibians and
                                Reptiles,1994.
        Check availability   Santa Fe/Gainesville 3rd Floor SF 515 .C36 1994
              at

5 ☐ THE CARE OF   Title The care of reptiles and amphibians in captivity /
     REPTILES AND   Author Mattison, Christopher.
     AMPHIBIANS   Published London :Blandford ; New York, N.Y. :Distributed in the U.S. by Sterling
     IN CAPTIVITY   Pub. Co.,1992.

broaden the search beyond turtles and reptiles. However, one of them ("captive reptiles") appears especially promising. "Captive" expands the search beyond "pets," but "reptiles" remains focused on the specific type of animals that are the subject of the project.

Clicking on a subject hyperlink takes the researcher to a listing of all of the titles in that category **(see Figure 3.6)**, revealing sources that haven't been located in previous searches. Even better, many of these texts seem more narrowly focused on diseases, medical treatments, and health issues of reptiles, indicating that they will likely provide the most useful information.

Depending on how specific your keyword terms are at the beginning of a search, you might repeat this narrowing-down process a number of times to locate your best sources.

Ensure the Quality of the Research Sources

Academic researchers need to evaluate the "backgrounds" of potential sources of information to screen out unsuitable or untrustworthy sources and to identify those that are most appropriate and credible.

A number of criteria are traditionally used to evaluate sources, including:

- Purpose
- Reputation
- Intended audience
- Reliability
- Timeliness

You will no doubt quickly discover that applying these criteria involves skills that take time and experience to develop. In some ways, learning to evaluate sources is like developing a proficiency in the arts. A music teacher can instruct you in the basics of playing the clarinet—show you which holes to cover to produce certain notes and how to shape your mouth to accommodate the mouthpiece and reed—but you must practise diligently to learn the subtle control required to make music rather than squawks. If you want to play a musical composition with extremely high notes, you will need to learn to make minute adjustments and refine these skills to produce the desired result.

Evaluating sources is much the same. There is no single feature of a source that demonstrates accuracy or appropriateness. Instead, you must analyze a variety of clues in relation to how you plan to use the information. If what you need are facts and statistics, then you will be especially concerned with accuracy, timeliness, and reliability of the source. If you need an opinion that supports a position, then you want to make sure the source is credible, reasonable, and authoritative. But if you are looking for firsthand experience that is persuasive because it is personal, then it might not matter if the author is renowned.

Most research projects use a mix of all these types of sources. A former student who had worked in a day care centre wanted to investigate how preschool children were affected by spending six to eight hours away from their parents. The final paper combined facts from recent psychological and sociological studies with the opinions of noted authorities on children and child care, as well as anecdotes from the students' own experiences.

As has already been mentioned, you can generally trust information housed in a library because it has undergone a great deal of evaluation. A number of controls ensure the quality of these sources. The author's colleagues, editors, and publishers have reviewed textbooks, scholarly studies, and articles in specialized journals. On the other hand, you should never accept a library source as credible or appropriate just because it is in the library. Keep in mind that information exists in all sorts of forms (stories, reports, arguments, statistics) and is published for a variety of purposes (to express a belief, to entertain, to persuade); therefore, it is important to determine whether a source is suitable for your intended use. *Moby Dick* contains a great deal of information about whales, but you probably wouldn't want to use Melville's novel as a source for a research paper on marine biology.

As stated, the library remains the best starting point for the novice researcher because you can have confidence in the reliability of its resources. Library systems have been developed to allow you to evaluate the quality of the resources. The format of the online catalogue provides you with much of the information you will need to determine the reliability of a text **(see Figure 3.7)**.

The World Wide Web is an entirely different matter. Often, novice researchers think that web pages must be reliable because they are current and public. ("People wouldn't publish inaccurate information publicly, would they?") However, unlike more traditional forms of information media (books, magazines, journals, and government or organization documents), no one regulates information published on the web, and there is no standard method of cataloguing information. Frequently the indicators needed for evaluation (authorship, date of publication, organizational affiliations) are missing. This poses unique problems for research that will be discussed more fully in Chapter 5. But before tackling those more complex situations, it makes sense to learn essential evaluation skills in the user-friendly online catalogue. After all, it's necessary to master the basics before attempting to hit a C above high G.

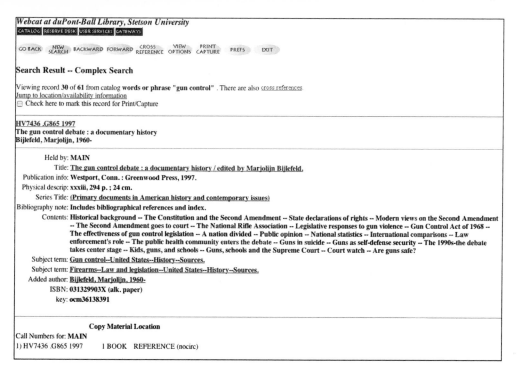

FIGURE 3.7

The listings in an online catalogue provide much of the information you will need to evaluate it (i.e., author, publisher, copyright date, whether it contains references, and a summary of the contents).

When my student was trying to decide whether to use Chris Mattison's text on the care of reptiles for her research project, she had to evaluate whether it was a worthwhile source. The book is part of our school library's holdings—a good sign, but would it be a suitable resource that fulfilled the academic requirements for a scholarly research essay? She needed to be suspicious and not accept this information at face value. So she asked questions.

What Is Its Purpose?

This is the first question you should ask when evaluating a potential source. Is the source attempting to persuade you to adopt an idea or belief? Is it someone's opinion? Is it a report on facts or findings? Is it an advertisement? All information has a purpose or a goal, and an enormous amount of information in our culture professes to be unbiased but contains a hidden (or not so hidden) agenda intended to persuade the reader.

If you are trying to decide between buying a Mitsubishi Eclipse or a Ford Mustang, you might visit dealers and obtain brochures. However, unless you are extremely inexperienced, you wouldn't limit yourself to the print and online brochures that a salesperson supplies. The purpose of these brochures is to sell cars. Although the facts they contain might be accurate, they are intended to give you the most favourable impression of a vehicle.

Most of these publications are carefully contrived to leave you feeling as if your life would be wretched and empty if you did *not* purchase the vehicle. If you want a more accurate picture of how these two cars compare—one that takes limitations as well as advantages into account—you need to refer to *Consumer Reports* or some other less-biased source for information **(see Figure 3.8)**.

What Is Its Bias?

Even a biased source can be valuable to your research, but only if you recognize its slant. Some writers (published authors as well as students!) are so intent on persuading readers

FIGURE 3.8

This website presents information that enables consumers to compare the price and features of vehicles.

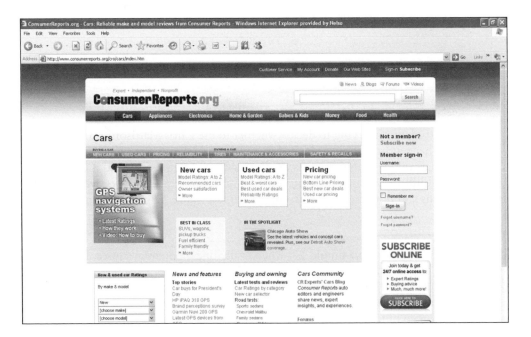

to agree with their opinions that they misrepresent facts or ignore information that challenges their conclusions. Like the car dealer, they want to sell you on an idea without considering other options. To accept what these writers say as unequivocally true will only result in repeating their error.

Objectivity and balance are distinguishing features of good academic research. A scholarly source will frequently present opinion, but intellectuals are committed to reasoned argumentation that considers (rather than ignores or withholds) conflicting viewpoints. Of course, some topics (such as abortion, capital punishment, and gay marriage) have elicited such extensive, heated, and polarized debate—even within scholarly circles—that the only way you will arrive at a balanced understanding is to read widely, becoming familiar with arguments on both sides of the divide.

A sarcastic or superior tone is frequently a sign of bias. Rather than draw on established facts and reasonable argument, writers with strong bias frequently resort to rude put-downs to discredit contradictory views. Television and radio talk shows have made us all too accustomed to this type of discourse. However, if the author of a source sounds like he or she could be a guest on a show hosted by Jerry Springer, Montel Williams, or Howard Stern, there is good reason to be skeptical. Scholarly writing relies on reason rather than ridicule to make its points. If you are already familiar with your topic, you might recognize serious omissions or distortions. But what if you are unsure whether the writer has been fair? The only way to allay your uncertainty is to run further background checks.

Where Does It Come From?

One way to determine whether a source is legitimate is identify who published it. One of my students recently wrote a research paper on privatized health care. His bibliography listed numerous publications, but the Fraser Institute (<www.fraserinstitute.org>) had published all of them. This "think tank" has an overtly business-oriented agenda (tagline: "A free and prosperous world through choice, markets and responsibility"), as well as strong ties to conservative and business interests in Canada. It therefore can hardly be expected to present all sides of this important issue. The information contained in its publications might be technically correct, but the organization's agenda will necessarily shape the argument in explicit and implicit ways. If the publisher is a university press, a well-established publishing company, or a government agency, then you can have greater confidence in the objectivity of the source (see Figure 3.9). These organizations carefully examine and review information before affixing their names (and their reputations) to it. If the source is published by an organization, then you need to carefully review its goals and methods of quality control.

FIGURE 3.9

You can be reasonably confident in the accuracy and objectivity of this source on the private health care issue because it was compiled by an organization with a commitment to objectivity.

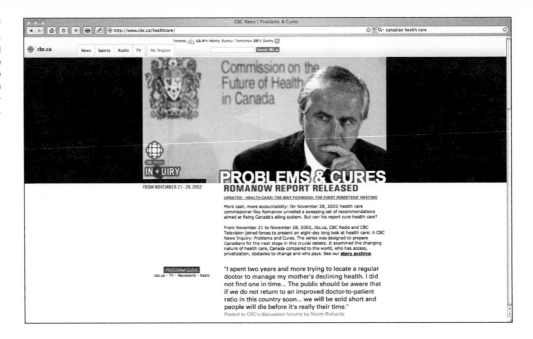

Blandford Press published the book about reptiles that my student was considering using for her research project. This publishing company was unfamiliar to both of us. Therefore, she conducted a quick search on the Internet using the search engine *Google*.

TIP

Internet search engines are discussed at length in Chapter 5. *Google* is a good choice for this search because "Blandford Press" is a very distinctive search term. Notice that this multiword search term is enclosed in quotation marks to indicate that both words should appear as a phrase.

She wasn't able to locate a company website, but the search revealed numerous books published by Blandford (many of which dealt with reptiles and birds) that had been included in bibliographies compiled by reputable organizations **(see Figure 3.10)**. This reassured her that the publisher was credible.

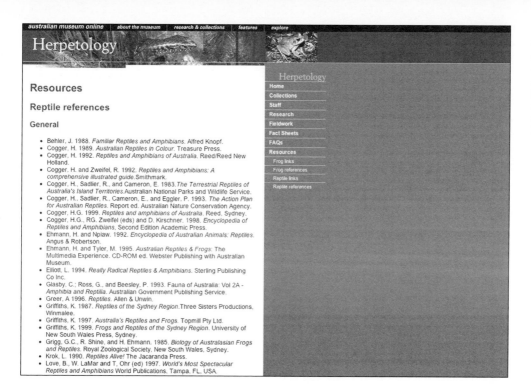

FIGURE 3.10

The results of an Internet search for "Blandford Press" included this site from the Australian Museum that includes a bibliography of credible and helpful sources about herpetology. Mattison's book is included in the list.

Even if you know that the publishing company is experienced and responsible, you still need to confirm that the author is an authority on the subject (i.e., has the necessary education and/or credentials). One way to verify an author's qualifications is by determining which organizations or institutions he or she is affiliated with. Often a brief biography is included in the publication itself. (Refer to *Biography Index* if in doubt.) You might also conduct an author search in the online catalogue to determine whether he or she has published other books or articles on the subject.

Determining the credentials of the author is especially important when you are evaluating articles in mainstream periodicals. Even though many news magazines (e.g., *Maclean's, Newsweek, Saturday Night*) provide accurate information, they are usually not the best source of information for academic papers. This is because the authors of these are not experts on the subjects, but journalists who work under very short time-lines. They conduct research and interview experts, but they are rarely themselves authorities on the subject.

For instance, in her pet turtle research, my student located a newspaper article about how to prevent the spread of salmonella. However, when she did an Internet search of the author's name, she discovered that the reporter usually wrote restaurant and food reviews. The information in the article is probably accurate, and although the author might be an authority on the tastiest turtle soup in town, she is clearly not an expert on bacteriology. This is why you should locate scholarly journals that contain information written and reviewed by experts rather than reporters.

An author search using the online catalogue revealed that the library owns 15 books on reptiles authored by Mattison. A subsequent Internet search revealed that he is a zoologist who has also published numerous journal articles and is an acknowledged expert on wildlife.

Who Is the Audience?

Just as it is important to determine a publisher's and author's credentials, so too it is necessary to consider the intended audience of a source. In fact, many choices you make in everyday life are governed by this principle. When baby-sitting your four-year-old nephew, you might rent *Finding Nemo* to entertain him, but if you popped *Finding Nemo* into the DVD player on a first date, you'd probably find you have a lot more Friday nights free for baby-sitting. When evaluating a source, the key principle is that the information must not be too simple (or too technical) for an educated adult audience.

For instance, the keyword search for "reptiles AND pets" produced a text that lists *Juvenile literature* as one of its subject categories **(see Figure 3.11)**. Obviously this work was written for children. Once again, the full-display listing found in the online catalogue provides clues that enable the astute researcher to eliminate inappropriate sources.

At the same time, you can't rely on receiving such obvious clues in all cases. For that reason, it is important to pay attention to the vocabulary of the source and its attention to detail. Encyclopedia articles generally provide information that is technically correct, but these articles are probably not suitable sources for post-secondary-level research papers. This is because encyclopedias target a very general (rather than a scholarly) audience, and they tend to summarize rather than elaborate on a topic.

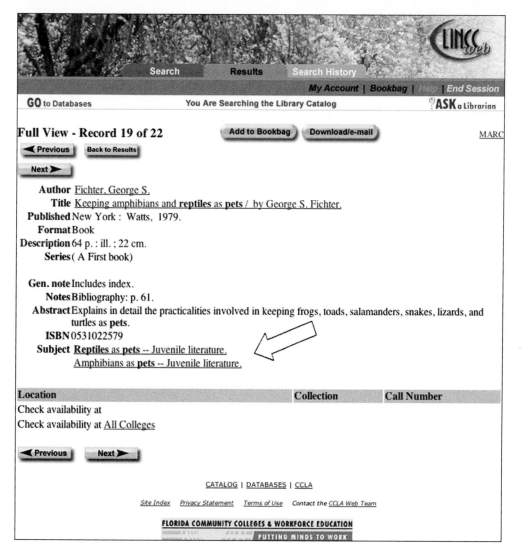

FIGURE 3.11

The online index clearly indicates that this book was written for children and would be too elementary for a postsecondary research project.

On the other hand, you also need to eliminate sources that are too technical or specialized. For her "turtle law" project, my student realized she needed to understand more about the transmission and treatment of salmonella. One search uncovered a 40-page article that argued "gram-negative bacteria do not 'secrete' proteins into their environment but only export proteins in their strategic periplasm."[1] There was no question about the accuracy and academic reliability of this source, but it was so full of medical jargon and technical information that she could hardly read it, much less understand it enough to incorporate it effectively in her own writing.

When Was It Produced?

For many research projects, the more up-to-date the information is, the better. Because knowledge is constantly being created and revised, you must carefully note when information was created and determine if it is still valuable. Depending on your topic, you may want to limit your search to information produced in the past 5 or 10 years. If you are interested in some discipline in which information is quickly outdated (such as genetic research), information even a year old may be too old.

On the other hand, because something was produced many years ago doesn't necessarily mean it is irrelevant. Even if your topic deals with a rapidly changing field, such as technology, an older text might be valuable. If you were investigating the history of the development of artificial intelligence, you might be interested in reading a report by Thomas Watson, a former chairman of IBM. In 1943 Watson declared, "I think there is a world market for maybe five computers." Likewise, the proceedings of the 1977 Convention of the World Future Society might prove pertinent. At this gathering of forward-looking "techies" Kenneth H. Olson, president of DEC (a leader in computer sales that in the 1960s produced the first small computer to be sold on a retail basis), announced, "There is no reason for any individual to have a computer in his home." The expectations of these pioneers of the computer industry form a striking contrast with current attitudes and practices. Depending on your topic, even a text written in another century might prove valuable.

---

1. Cornelis, Guy R., and Van Gijsegem, Frédérique. "Assembly and Function of Type III Secretory Systems." Annual Review of Microbiology 54 (2000): 735-74. Academic Search Premier. EBSCOHost. Seminole Community College Library. 3 Jan. 2006.

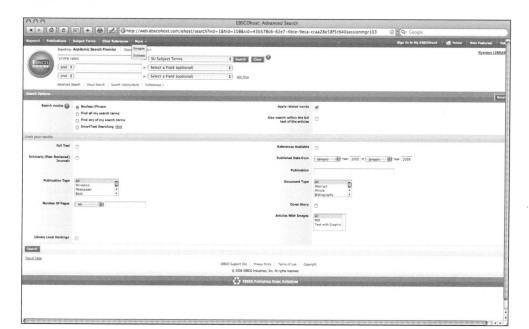

FIGURE 3.12

The use of limiting publication
dates in a library search.

TIP

» **Searching by Publication Date**

Many library search tools allow you to limit your search to a particular time period **(see
Figure 3.12)**. This allows you to refine your search even further to eliminate inappropriate
sources. If your online catalogue doesn't have a place in the search window to enter "year"
or "publication year," check to see if there is an "advanced search" window that does.

Nonetheless, for many research topics the most current information is the most desirable.
For this reason, you need to pay attention to copyright dates. Mattison's book was published
in 1992. Because it is over 17 years old, it doesn't offer the most current knowledge on the
topic. However, this doesn't mean it won't be a useful source. All the same, this student was
cautious about her use of this text and made sure that she located other, more recently
published resources to verify some of the scientific information.

What Does It Look Like?

It is a well-known fact that the best way to learn to detect counterfeit money is to study the genuine article. Once you become familiar with the appearance, colouring, and texture of real bills, you will immediately spot a false one. For the same reason, starting in an academic library where so much of the information bears the marks of authenticity and reliability will help you recognize suitable sources.

Scholarly work looks serious. By this I mean that it may contain illustrations, graphs, or charts, but it will rarely have glossy, flashy photos designed to appeal to a mass audience. The language used assumes an educated readership. These sources don't talk down to the reader; instead, they employ the language used by experts in the field.

Most importantly, a scholarly work offers various forms of corroboration to confirm its credibility. It will support any claims made with statistics and information from other sources. Look for footnotes and parenthetical citations within the text as well as an index, works cited, or bibliography section in the back. Again, the full-text display of the online catalogue often will help you determine whether your text has the proper "pedigree" required of a scholarly text. The catalogue record of Mattison's book refers to a bibliography and an index **(see Figure 3.13)**. The proper documentation of supporting sources is fundamental to academic writing. (You should remember this when you produce your own research project!)

What Do Others Say About It?

A recommendation is an important tool in evaluation. When Roger Ebert and Richard Roeper both give an enthusiastic "thumbs up" to a new movie, you are more likely to head to the theatre. Similarly, reviews and recommendations of research sources are another way to evaluate the merit of a source. If it has been recommended by an instructor or cited in another reputable source, you can usually trust that it is credible. Frequently library search tools provide information about the text (a summary, abstract, or listing of the contents) that allows you to better assess whether a resource is appropriate. The full-text display of Mattison's book indicates that there is a bibliography and index. It also contains a very detailed listing of the contents of the book **(see Figure 3.13)**.

Full View - Record 13 of 22 Add to Bookbag | Download/e-mail | MARC

Previous | Back to Results | Next

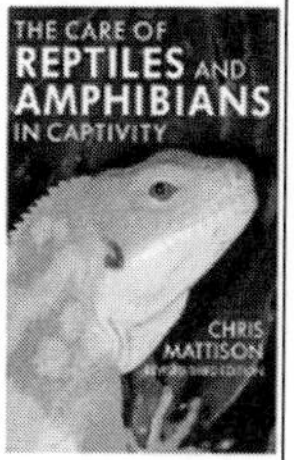

Author Mattison, Christopher.
Title The care of **reptiles** and amphibians in captivity / Chris Mattison.
Edition Rev. 3rd ed.
Published London : Blandford ; New York, N.Y. : Distributed in the U.S. by Sterling Pub. Co., 1992.
Format Book
Description 317 p., [16] p. of plates : ill. (some col.) ; 22 cm.

Notes Includes bibliographical references (p. 303-306) and indexes.
Contents General care -- Some biological considerations -- Thermoregulation; social behaviour -- Obtaining specimens and making a start -- Selecting species; legal aspects; selecting specimens; preparations -- Accommodation -- Cages; equipment -- Creating the right environment -- Temperature control; lighting control; humidity control; control of biological factors; the planted vivarium -- Foods and feeding -- Vegetable food; animal food; supplements; methods of feeding; water; overfeeding -- Breeding -- Sex determination; conditioning; stimuli; mating; pregnancy; parturition; egg-laying; incubation; rearing young; breeding programmes -- Diseases -- Controlling diseases; environmental diseases; nutritional diseases; bacterial infections; protozoan infections; endoparasites; ectoparasites; fungal infections; miscellaneous disorders -- Handling -- Descriptions of species and their maintenance -- Caudata: newts and salamanders -- Ambystomidae: Mole salamanders -- Salamandridae -- Plethodontidae: Woodland salamanders -- Anura: frogs and toads -- Pipidae: tongueless frogs.
(cont) Discoglossidae: fire-bellied toads, painted frog and midwife toad -- Pelobatidae: spadefoot toads -- Ranidae -- Raninae: true frogs -- Mantellinae -- Dendrobatidae: poison arrow frogs -- Rhacophoridae -- Microhylidae -- Bufonidae: true toads -- Hylidae: tree-frogs -- Leptodactylidae -- Crocodilia: crocodiles and alligators -- Chelonia: turtles and tortoises -- Pelomedusidae -- Chelidae: side-necked turtles -- Chelydridae: mud, musk and snapping turtles -- Emydidae: freshwater turtles -- Testudinidae: land tortoises -- Trionychidae: soft-shelled turtles -- Squamata: sub-order lacertilia: lizards -- Gekkonidae: geckos -- Eublepharinae -- Sphaerodactylinae -- Gekkoninae -- Xantusidae: night lizards -- Iguanidae: iguanas -- Agamidae: agamas -- Chamaeleontidae: chameleons -- Scincidae: skinks -- Cordylidae: zonures -- Gerrhosauridae: plated lizards -- Lacertidae -- Teiidae: tegus and whiptails -- Anguidae: slow-worms, glass lizards and alligator lizards -- Varanidae: monitors -- Amphisbaenidae -- Squamata: sub-order serpentes: snakes -- Typhlopidae and leptotyphlopidae: blind snakes.

FIGURE 3.13

This book includes a bibliography and an index, indications that this is a scholarly work.

Summary

Key Factors of Source Evaluation

What is the purpose of the document?

- Does it present fact, opinion, or both?

Does it maintain a fair, balanced, and reasonable perspective?

- Where does the document come from?
- Who is the publisher?
- Who is the author?

For whom is the document intended?

- Is it written for a scholarly, post-secondary-level audience?
- Is it too technical or specific for your project?

When was the document published?

- Does it include the most up-to-date information available?
- If dated, does it offer an interesting perspective or point of contrast?

What does the document look like?

- Does it look serious and scholarly?
- Does it have footnotes, a bibliography, an index, and other signs of credibility?

What do others say about the document?

- Has it been recommended by an instructor or cited in another, credible source?
- Is there a review of the source in an abstract or summary?

EXERCISES

1. Your sociology teacher has assigned a paper on "hate speech on the Internet." Compose a list of research questions that will help you focus this topic.

2. Review the research questions you composed in Exercise 1 and list the types of information (e.g., facts? statistics? opinions of experts? definitions? eyewitness or personal

testimony? a combination of some or all of these?) you will need to fulfill this assignment. Indicate, as well, the types of sources (e.g., books, periodicals, surveys, interviews, websites) that you think might be fruitful places to look for this kind of information.

3. Access your school's online catalogue, and conduct a *keyword* search (make sure you click on the appropriate "search type") using the phrase " 'hate speech' AND Internet" (remember to enclose multiword search terms in quotation marks and capitalize the Boolean "AND"). Choose two of the results that seem most relevant to the assignment, and list of all of the Library of Congress subject categories under which these sources are catalogued.

4. From the two sources you selected in Exercise 3, choose the one you consider to be the best match for this topic. Using the "Key Factors of Source Evaluation" listed in this chapter, write a paragraph in which you detail why this source is/is not a credible and appropriate source of information for the assignment mentioned in Exercise 1.

 5. If you are using the InfoTrac College Edition database in your course, use the passcode provided with this textbook to access the database and conduct a "Keyword" search (check the appropriate term immediately under the search phrase window) for the phrase " 'hate speech' AND Internet." Choose the result that appears most relevant. Using the "Key Factors of Source Evaluation" and the suggestions for determining the origins of a source listed in this chapter, write a paragraph in which you detail why this source is/is not a credible and appropriate source of information for the assignment mentioned in Exercise 1.

 6. Using the same source you chose in Exercise 5, click on the box marked "Link" in the left margin and a list of related topics will appear. Choose two of these related topics and (in a sentence or two) explain how these topics are pertinent to the assignment outlined in Exercise 1.

4

Get Immediate Results: Library Databases

"As a general rule the most successful man in life is the man who has the best information."

BENJAMIN DISRAELI

Although I am a bit troubled by his gendered language (Disraeli made his statement in an age less concerned with inclusiveness), for the researcher, his sentiment certainly holds true. The aim of this chapter is to help you acquire the best information. Given that we live in "The Information Age," this might not seem to be such a difficult task. After all, as mentioned throughout this book, the Internet has made an enormous amount of information available to anyone with a dial-up or broadband connection. But the operative word here is *best*. Note that Disraeli didn't link success to volume—he linked it to quality. The successful researcher is adept at rejecting unreliable and/or unverifiable information in favour of that which is "best"—trustworthy, reliable, and relevant.

For this reason, we initially focused our attention on the library. In fact, until now, the only research tool discussed at length has been the online catalogue. Those of you who regularly surf the web may have experienced moments of frustration. You may even have been impatient enough to skip ahead. Compared to the split-second access of the web, using the online catalogue seems relatively complex and slow way to get what you want. Although the catalogue identifies potential sources, you still need to physically find the texts and check them out. There is, however, a library tool that provides immediate access to information in a way that is reminiscent of the World Wide Web. That tool is the full-text database. In fact, students sometimes confuse databases with web pages because the information they provide is so instantaneous. Databases are likely to be one of the most important resources you'll use as a researcher; through them you can acquire some of the *best* information available on your topic—information you'll need to become a successful researcher.

What Is a Database?

A database, simply put, is a collection of computer data that has been arranged so that it can be easily retrieved. Computers are great organizers. In fact, you probably have used a computer at home or at work for just this purpose. Many businesses, for example, usually keep information about customers in a database so they can access it in a number of different ways (according to last name, phone number, address, etc.). When used in reference to library research, however, the term "database" refers to a very specific tool.

Library databases come in two basic varieties: **bibliographic** and **full-text**. A bibliographic database will provide you with access to a description of an article (or other source of information). A full-text database provides you with access to the entire article. You can read the material on your computer monitor, print it, or save it to retrieve at a later time.

T I P

The distinction between bibliographic material and the genuine document is important. Sometimes students will cite a bibliographic index or an abstract from a bibliography on their Works Cited pages. In order to include a resource in your project, you must track down (and cite) the actual article.

In recent years, many databases have been produced that are a combination of both bibliographic and full-text entries. A search will produce results that include both full-text articles as well as bibliographic information about pertinent articles (often with abstracts) that you must locate elsewhere **(see Figure 4.1)**.

Bibliographic Databases

A bibliographic database is simply an electronic version of a bibliographic index. You are probably familiar with the bibliographies at the conclusion of a book or article (you even may have been required to include one at the conclusion of a term paper). In these instances, a bibliography is an alphabetical listing of all of the sources a writer has consulted or cited in his or her work.

You may not realize, however, that there are many different types of bibliographies. (The *Readers' Guide to Periodical Literature* is one.) Some of these bibliographies are general in nature and they index documents on a broad range of topics. Many are devoted to specific disciplines. Print bibliographies, which you will find in the reference section of

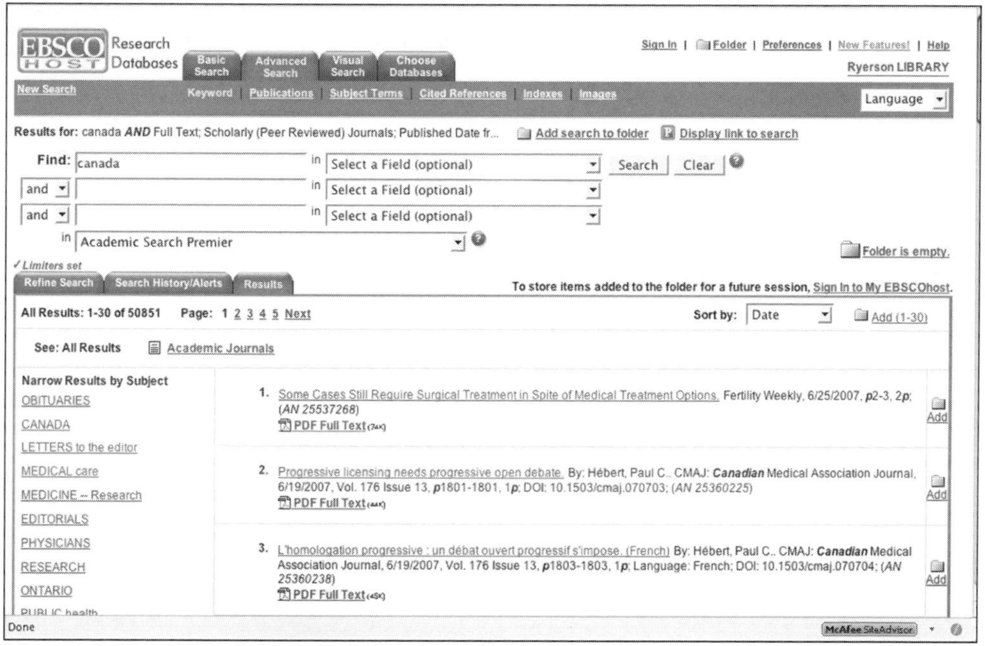

FIGURE 4.1

This database provides a combination of bibliographic/full-text results. Notice that entries that are available in full text are indicated (e.g., PDF, as in this example, or HTML Full Text). The other hits in this list must be accessed by other means (e.g., interlibrary loan).

your library, are typically huge multivolume works with very small type and are usually published annually to catalogue all of the documents published that year. To use these hard-copy versions, you must look up your key term or phrase in each volume—working year-by-year through the set.

The electronic versions are much more user-friendly. They allow you to search all of the records (regardless of the year of publication) simultaneously. Be advised, however, that most databases only go back as far as the mid-1970s, and some only to the mid-1980s, as most libraries have not digitized their materials before these dates. If you want to locate texts that were published earlier than this, you will usually have to use the printed volumes.

These bibliographic indices operate a lot like the library catalogue. They help you discover documents (frequently articles in periodicals, but sometimes government documents, essays, or chapters in books, etc.), but you still need to locate the texts themselves to access this information. Because they are library tools, these bibliographic databases are designed with research in mind: They allow you to locate information according to subject, author, title, or publisher.

FIGURE 4.2

This database provides
bibliographic information as
well as an extensive abstract,
or summary, of the article. All
of this information can help
you evaluate, as well as locate,
the text; however, it does *not*
provide the full text of the
article.

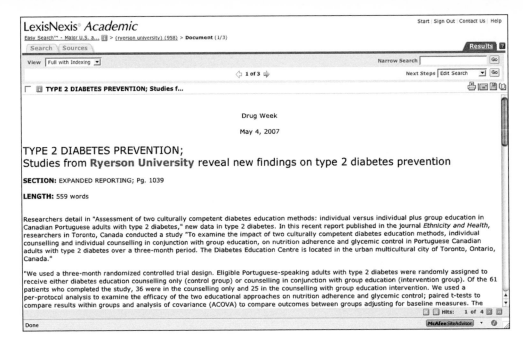

Often they provide excellent "abstracts," or summaries, of the articles that permit you to evaluate the contents quickly without having to read the entire article **(see Figure 4.2)**.

Like their hard-copy cousins, bibliographic databases are usually organized according to specific disciplines or interests. For example, the *Arts & Humanities Citation Index* indexes articles in major arts and humanities journals as well as relevant items from leading science and social science periodicals. *Federal Publication Locator* is an index of Canadian federal government publications (<www.collectionscanada.gc.ca/7/5/index-e.html>). The *Book Review Digest* provides citations and reviews of current English-language fiction and nonfiction books.

Full-Text Databases

The other type of database is the full-text database. The full-text database is similar in many ways to the bibliographic database. The screen interface and features are similar to the bibliographic database, and it provides a citation as well as an abstract or summary. However, it also provides you with the complete document, online.

The most common type of research resource available in full text is **periodicals**. Full-text databases provide instantaneous access from one's home or office to numerous newspapers, magazines, and scholarly or professional journals—publications that are published on a daily, weekly, or monthly schedule.

You'll recall that periodicals are vital to many research projects for a number of reasons. First, they are published more quickly than books, so the information in a journal article is often more current than what you will find on your library shelves. Second, articles that appear in academic and professional journals (as opposed to popular magazines) are frequently written by experts and reviewed by other experts in a field, making them very credible and authoritative sources. Third, they also tend to be more focused than books, rarely exceeding 25 to 30 pages in length. Books, on the other hand, are frequently 200 pages (or more). Fourth, although books often provide indices in the back to help pinpoint specific pages for particular facts, you sometimes need to page through a lot of extraneous information to find what you need. In many instances, all you really require is one chapter. If you have limited the scope of your search by posing specific research questions (see Chapter 3), you have a definite idea of what you are looking for. For this reason, it often takes less time to locate what you are looking for in a periodical than in a book.

Although most libraries (public as well as academic) subscribe to major news and popular-interest periodicals (e.g., *Maclean's, Newsweek, The Economist*), until recently, only libraries at large universities could afford to subscribe to and house many of the academic journals available. This meant that if you were enrolled at a smaller school with limited holdings, the only way you could acquire an article from some journals was through a lengthy interlibrary loan process that often took four to six weeks. Today, almost all public and school libraries subscribe to numerous databases, increasingly the full-text variety. As a result, no matter how limited a library's physical resources may be, it can now offer 24-hour access to journals and periodicals that were once available only at major research institutions.

Get to Know Your Databases

Because libraries make independent decisions about which databases they will purchase, it is impossible to predict what you will encounter at your particular school or public library. However, there are a number of databases that, like the chain stores you encounter in virtually every mall across Canada (The Gap, Body Shop, Starbucks, etc.), are perennial favourites.

Often, libraries will purchase a package deal from a database provider. These are actually database "libraries" that feature numerous databases, some bibliographic, some full text.

InfoTrac College Edition, OCLC, EBSCOhost, Gale, and Lexis-Nexis are examples of database publishers that provide databases either singly or in groupings. Deciphering your library's holdings can be a bit confusing at first because some databases can be purchased as either bibliographic or full text. In fact, purchasing a database is a bit like buying a car—some things are standard equipment, but there are a lot of options to choose from as well. For that reason, you might encounter similarly named databases in slightly altered forms in different libraries.

Please note, as well, that the more general database services will provide access to some of the same material. For example, you will likely be able to access *The Economist,* a very popular weekly publication, through a number of the database services.

Access to the Database: On-site or Remote

The first thing you need to determine is how to access your library's databases. Libraries pay a lot of money to subscribe to a database, so they almost always limit access to enrolled students (or cardholders in the case of public libraries). Some libraries limit access by making the databases available only through on-campus computer terminals (sometimes referred to as an intranet or LAN). This means that you can use a database only if you are on campus. An increasing number of libraries make it possible for students to access a database through a password-protected link to the library website. By making databases available via the Internet, these libraries have truly "gone virtual." If you are working on a paper at two in the morning (and many of my students swear they do their best work at that hour) and discover you need an additional source or further information, you can point your browser at your library's website and find what you need. You are no longer limited by library hours or physical access, for you can locate full-text academic articles from your home computer.

Schools use different methods to provide remote access to the library systems. Some schools link a student's school-issued identification to the library system. Others link the student's university email (student@university.ca) to the library system. Contact your library if you have any questions. Also, with this text you may have received a subscription to InfoTrac College Edition, a full-text database that is available 24/7 for your research needs.

Search Tips When Using Databases

All of the research strategies we have discussed so far *also* apply to using library databases. Like the online catalogue, a full-text database is a stocked pond. The documents you locate using a database are previously published (and therefore regulated and reviewed) articles.

Because it uses an electronic search tool (like the online catalogue), a database allows you to find a "perfect match" by using the keywords and phrases you have discovered while converting your topic into research questions (see Chapter 2) and following the leads revealed by your online catalogue's subject category hyperlinks (see Chapter 3). However, understanding a few subtle differences will make your searches more effective.

TIP

» **Citations for Electronic Documents**

Many of the documents contained in a full-text database were originally published in print format. As such, they require a special format for citation that indicates that you accessed them via a database. See the documentation sections on this book's companion website (<www.digitalresearch.nelson.com>) for more information.

As mentioned in Chapters 2 and 3, the online catalogue typically uses Library of Congress subject categories for classifying print materials. This means that the keywords and phrases that immediately come to mind might not be the most successful search words. (Remember the student who couldn't locate any documents using the search terms "turtles AND salmonella," but who found excellent resources when she used the terms "reptiles AND pets" and "captive reptiles"?) This is because the online catalogue cannot electronically search word-by-word through all of the books on your library's shelves. Instead, when books are catalogued in the library, they are categorized according to established subject headings; you must identify these to access the best information on your topic.

Bibliographic databases operate much the same way. When the information about a particular document is entered (such as author, title, publication information), it is also classified with relevant subject categories (often called "descriptors" or "identifiers") that help you locate the document using a subject or keyword search **(see Figure 4.3)**. Be advised that the categories in bibliographic databases are frequently different from Library of Congress terms. Sometimes it takes a little trial and error to discover which terms work best.

FIGURE 4.3

Like the online reference catalogue, the "subject" categories (sometimes called "descriptors") are hyperlinks. If this article is a good resource, you might be able to link to other documents that address your topic.

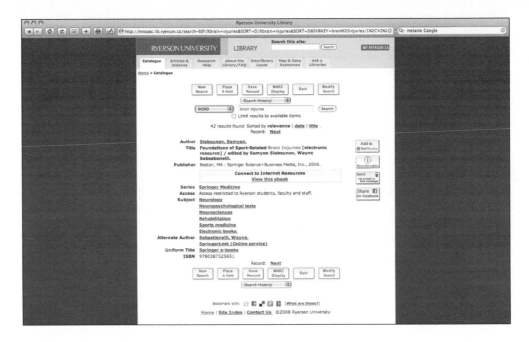

Using "Advanced Search"

Because the documents in a full-text database are recorded entirely digital, database search engines can normally conduct a word-by-word search through each text. This may require that you use the "advanced search" option and/or check a special box before conducting a search **(see Figure 4.4)**.

Because a match is made if a keyword appears anywhere in the wording of the document, a search term that was unsuccessful in the online catalogue or a bibliographic database might work in a full-text database. This may seem fairly simple, but it actually puts a great deal of pressure on you to be precise in how you phrase your searches (and spell your search terms). Remember the tips about multiword and Boolean search phrases (see Chapter 2)? For instance, a full-text database search using the phrase "school violence" returned only 24 hits (because the search engine was looking for the phrase "school violence"). On the other hand, a search using the same tool for "school AND violence" resulted in approximately 3,400 matches.

FIGURE 4.4

"Basic Search" provides the user with limited capabilities to define the search.

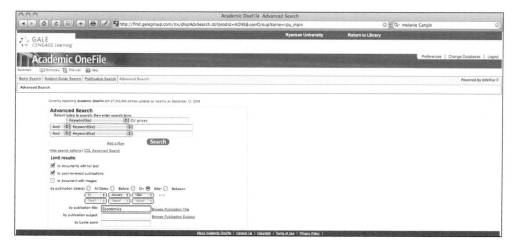

FIGURE 4.5

Using the "Advanced Search" mode, it is possible to search the entire text of a document for the search phrase; results can also be limited to full-text documents (if the database includes both bibliographic and full-text entries). You can further limit your search by publication type and date.

Most databases offer the option of conducting either a basic or advanced search. The advanced search mode features alternatives for refining your search and limiting your results. Most advanced search modes permit you to search the entire text of the document, limit your results to full-text documents, narrow your search to certain types of publications (e.g., journals or newspapers), and restrict the date of publication to a particular time period.

The advanced search mode also allows you to refine other aspects of your search, thus limiting your results to the most pertinent sources **(see Figure 4.5)**. If your research requires the most up-to-date sources, you can limit your search to the past year or two. Some instructors require that your research include different types of publications. The advanced search mode permits you to restrict your search to specific types of publications (e.g., articles from newspapers or journals). Most importantly, if you are looking for instant gratification and the database you are using includes both bibliographic and full-text entries, it is possible to limit your results to only full-text articles.

Like other electronic library tools, full-text databases enable you to be a "research sleuth," for they provide a way for you to connect with relevant resources (see Chapter 3). Once you locate a promising source, explore these possibilities by clicking on the identifiers or descriptors that hyperlink to lists of other related documents **(see Figure 4.6)**.

If you get an overwhelming number of matches for a keyword(s) search in a database, use your sleuthing skills. Quickly scan the titles until you locate an article that appears relevant. Read the abstract or summary to confirm your hunch, and if the article proves promising, notice the descriptors or indicators listed. Click on these hyperlinks to locate more articles like the one you have chosen.

FIGURE 4.6

The abstract reveals that this is a pertinent source, and the "Subject Terms" hyperlinks indicate other search phrases (AUDIOMETRY | LETTERS to the editor) that could lead to more valuable resources.

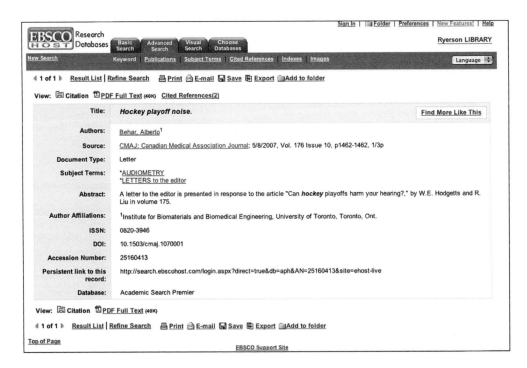

FIGURE 4.7

A full-text database provides you with a reprint of the complete article (including information about where it was previously published).

Of course, the beauty of full-text databases is that when you click on the hyperlink to view the "full text," up pops the complete article **(see Figure 4.7)**. You can print it out or read it online. One potential drawback to full-text databases is their limited coverage—most include articles printed only in the last 20 to 30 years, and none will include every article, no matter how relevant. However, the best databases continue to expand their coverage, increasing their holdings regularly.

EXERCISES

1. Locate the databases to which your school library subscribes. In a sentence or two, note how many of these databases provide full-text documents, and give the name of one or two general full-text databases that provide access to high-quality sources for a research project. In addition, note the name of a specialized bibliographic or full-text database that relates to your major or your educational interests.

2. Access one of the full-text databases you mentioned in Exercise 1 and conduct a keyword search for the phrase "salmonella AND reptiles." From the results list, choose the one you consider to be the most credible and appropriate source, and either print out or copy all of the bibliographic information (author, title of article, original source of publication, copyright date, page numbers) pertaining to it. Then write a paragraph explaining why you chose this source (based on your evaluation of the bibliographic information).

3. Because they contain electronic documents, full-text databases can search in a variety of ways, and this can produce different results. If you are using the InfoTrac College Edition database in your course, use the passcode provided with this text to access the database. From the menu on the left, select "Keyword search," type in the search phrase "salmonella AND reptiles"; click in the dot below the search phrase that states "in title, citation, abstract"; and click on "search." Write down the number of hits you receive. Conduct a second search with the same phrase, but this time click on the dot that states, "in entire article content." Write down the number of hits you obtain in this search, and then write a short explanation of why these numbers are different.

4. This chapter began with a quotation about how success is tied to acquiring the best information. The advanced search feature in InfoTrac College Edition can limit your search to only the best sources. In the menu on the left, click on "Start Over." Then click on "Advanced Search" (also on the left). From the drop-down menu that says "Select Index (Optional)," click on "Text Word (tx)," and enter the search phrase "salmonella AND reptiles." Then click on the box under the words "Limit the Current Search (Optional)" that states, "to refereed publications." (Refereed publications undergo a great deal of evaluation and thus are extremely credible.) Your results will appear when you click on the hyperlink "View" under "History." Write a brief comparison between these results and the results you received from the searches in Exercise 3.

PART
2

RESEARCH USING THE WORLD WIDE WEB

5 The Allure of the Printed Word

"If you put garbage in a computer, nothing comes out but garbage. But this garbage, having passed through a very expensive machine, is somehow ennobled, and none dare criticize it."

ANONYMOUS

The printed word has a powerful allure. We tend to believe that if information has been published there must be some truth to it. If you doubt this, then the next time you are in line at the grocery store, try *not* to read the headlines of the three or four tabloids that scream for your attention. Even if you know that tabloids specialize in bizarre half-truths and fabrications, they are difficult to ignore. Not only do we all read these headlines (despite their dubious authority), many of us actually speculate whether there might be some truth to them. Is a certain multimillionaire addicted to painkillers? Could that TV actress be wasting away from anorexia? Did that dashing actor really murder his wife?

We hesitate to dismiss these trumped-up stories, in part because we have been trained to respect the printed word. Throughout our childhood we are taught to pay attention to books—to read, remember, and repeat what we find in them. Later, we learn that our society recognizes only written documents as legally binding. When we want to attest to the veracity of what we are saying, we "put it in writing." We know, intellectually, that the mere act of writing will not transform a falsehood into a truth. However, when we read a published document, there are powerful dynamics at work that can cause us to accept ideas we might otherwise reject. These dynamics can, sometimes for good reasons and sometimes for bad, also lead us to think that published opinions and ideas are better than our own.

For this reason, the Internet, in spite of the enormous advances it has made in the transmission of information, can pose many problems for the novice researcher. If the printed word is alluring, then the Internet (with text as well as graphics, moving images, and sounds) is seductive. Like the tabloids, it can blur the distinction between truth and fiction, between information and entertainment. And, unlike articles published in credible sources, material published on the web may not have withstood the critical scrutiny of expert review.

Libraries vs. the WWW

The previous chapters have focused on teaching basic research strategies using library tools. We did this for the same reason that an instructor has a student driver practise in the relatively safe confines of an empty parking lot. New drivers need to become comfortable with the equipment and basic skills required before heading out to face the baffling challenges of the highway. Now that you understand basic research skills, you're ready to venture out from the confines of the library to the unregulated "information superhighway."

Only a decade or so ago, student research was, for the most part, limited to printed media (books, newspapers, periodicals) that were carefully controlled. These controls determined who and what could be published. Today the World Wide Web has created a huge grab bag of potential sources. An Internet search might turn up precious sources of information, but it can just as likely lead you to low-quality information.

Nevertheless, despite its dangers and drawbacks, the WWW does allow access to information that may not be available through your school's library. Throughout this text I have cautioned you to be wary of the web, yet I spend many of my waking hours online. I use the web to locate information that aids me in my professional as well as personal life. To be frank, for some topics, unless you are attending a large research institution, the WWW might provide you with more current and extensive resources than your school library. If this is the case, the challenge you face is to locate sites from among the millions on the web that satisfy the rigorous requirements of verification and authentication required in academic research.

Academic Research on the Internet Must Be Authenticated

Academic research has strict rules to establish the reliability of information. You must be able to

- Demonstrate that your information is accurate

- Indicate where you found it

- Establish that the source is credible

Once you grasp the more demanding standards of academic research, you can begin to comprehend—and overcome—the problems presented by the World Wide Web.

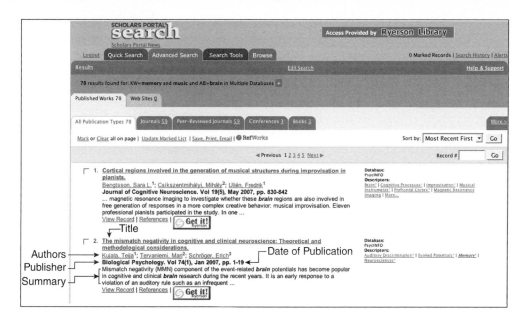

FIGURE 5.1

Library search tools include what you need to assess whether a source is credible and relevant. This entry from a database clearly indicates the author, publisher, date of publication, and a summary of the information contained in the article.

Because the standards for authenticating and documenting facts in academic research are more severe than those we employ in most everyday situations, library resources generally include only those sources that satisfy these more demanding standards. Online catalogues and subscription databases provide all of the information required to evaluate or verify the authority of a source **(see Figure 5.1)**. But unlike your library's digital resources, the web has no standardized system of organization or categorization. Internet search engines attempt to impose order on this chaos, but each has its own system of classification that affects the outcome of your search. In addition, the facts on web pages are not necessary validated so they might contain deceptive, biased, or incorrect information. And even when you locate a resource that is both pertinent and credible, the web page editor(s) might not include all of the information necessary to adequately document or confirm the source.

For these reasons, it will take all of your research skills to locate relevant and reliable sources on the Internet. It is critical that you:

- use search terms that will provide the best matches (see Chapter 2),
- explore the most promising locations, and
- evaluate (constantly) the quality of the information you find.

You might already be adept at navigating the web. And if you spend much time on the Internet, you have probably developed your own search strategies and a predisposition for certain search engines. It may seem to you that you already know enough to negotiate the demands of college research. Perhaps you do. However, you always need to keep in mind that when you are conducting research for an academic project, you must be *very selective.* When you are using the web, you must only cast your net into what I am calling "stocked ponds." Rather than using search tools that rely on computer robot programs to assign matches to your search terms, you need to use search guides that are highly evaluative and will lead you to web pages that fulfill the sophisticated requirements of academic research.

As Chapter 2 pointed out, most Internet search engines compile results by using computer "robots" or "spiders" that rank pages according to algorithmic programs. When you type in a search term, these robots look through the complete text of all the web pages in their collection of sites (no search engine currently searches *all* of the WWW) to find pages that include your term. This type of search, which normally doesn't take the context of your term into account, almost always retrieves an unmanageable number of results—and these are not necessarily in the best order for your particular needs.

A subject guide that has been compiled with scholarly research in mind—one that contains websites that take a careful and critical approach to academic subjects—is extremely valuable to the researcher who wants to use the Internet to locate resources. Such a guide provides access to a stocked pond—that is, to websites that have been appraised and judged current, credible, and relevant because they have been composed by reputable authors or organizations (refer to Figure 5.5 later in this chapter).

The most significant difference between regular search engines and subject guides or directories is that the former involve almost no human interaction, whereas the latter rely on a great deal of human selection and evaluation. Given the chaotic nature of the WWW, this assistance in evaluation can be invaluable. *Yahoo!,* one of the most widely used Internet guides, organizes its search mechanism around subject categories. Rather than simply matching terms, *Yahoo!* classifies the websites in its pool according to subject headings and returns results based on those headings. In fact, one of the reasons *Yahoo!* has become so popular is because searching by subject, rather than by exact terms, is—in many cases— more successful. When I was looking for a rocking chair for my front porch, I first tried a

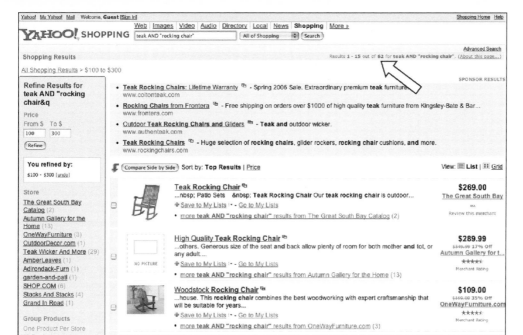

FIGURE 5.2

Using subject categories as a guide can help you narrow a search from almost 327,000 hits to 62.

search engine that strictly relied on matching terms. My search phrase, "rocking chair" returned over 48,000 matches, and most of these pages had nothing to do with purchasing a rocker. In *Yahoo!,* I was able to narrow my quest by choosing *shopping,* then *furniture,* then *outdoor furniture,* until I finally refined my search to what I was really looking for. At this point, *Yahoo!* retrieved 62 sites for me to review **(see Figure 5.2)**. Although these results are certainly more manageable, this experience illustrates another problem with Internet research: *Yahoo!'s* categories proved ultimately too limiting. Clearly, there are more than 62 online merchants that sell teak rocking chairs.

In the most basic sense, *Yahoo!'s* structure is similar to the classification system used in libraries. However, unlike the library, with its standardized Library of Congress subject headings, Internet subject guides adopt their own systems of categorization.

FIGURE 5.3

Using a basic search on *Google Scholar*, "Canada and Nursing," produced 372,000 references to scholarly journal articles, books, abstracts, and theses.

Yahoo! is an all-purpose subject directory that attempts to address the most common uses of the Internet. It handles communication, everyday questions, and e-commerce rather well because the majority of WWW users are most concerned with these applications. But *Yahoo!* hasn't been designed with academic research specifically in mind. Therefore, its subject headings and web page selections frequently are not well suited for the topics and disciplines involved in most college- or university-level research projects **(see Figure 5.3)**.

Google Scholar is another tool to consider. This search engine, a division of the larger Google service, identifies peer-reviewed papers, theses (by graduate students as part of their application to graduate), books, abstracts, and articles from a variety of sources. The results are ranked by a number of criteria including the full text of the article, the author, the publication in which the article belongs, and how often it is cited in other scholarly literature (see Google Scholar at <http://scholar.google.ca>).

TIP

It has become common practice for school libraries to create subject guides as part of their "virtual library" web pages. You would do well to check with a reference librarian about this, as librarians frequently consult with your professors when creating these subject guides. In fact, if your professor has a web page, he or she might have included a list of links that would be helpful in completing research assignments.

A number of subject guides have been expressly designed for academic research. These tools are aptly named "guides" because they steer users to the most appropriate sites and help them avoid inaccurate and/or unverifiable web pages. Nevertheless, it is important to remember that the same qualities that make these guides so valuable—the fact that they are limited in scope and compiled with a great deal of human evaluation—can sometimes be their greatest liabilities **(see Figures 5.4 and 5.5)**. The scope of some guides is limited and

FIGURE 5.4

This search, using the Boolean phrase "Canadian AND nursing" in the popular search engine *Yahoo!*, produced 1,260,000 hits. Reviewing this many web pages is an impossible task.

FIGURE 5.5

Frequently a *Google* search will take you to *Wikipedia,* an online encyclopedia. However, a disclaimer on the home page indicates that this site can be edited by anyone. Since information is only as credible as its source, I wouldn't recommend using this website for academic research.

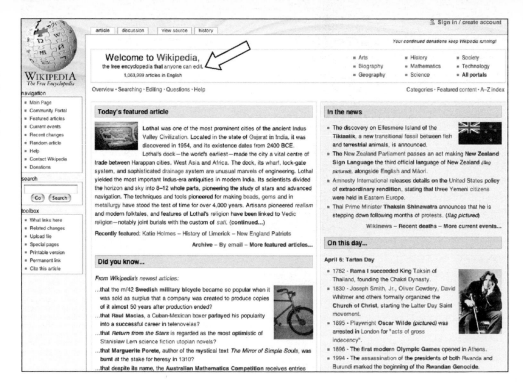

highly specialized and may reveal the limited perspective of individual human evaluators and compilers.

Moreover, because these guides are designed to be research tools, they often are modelled after library resources. Frequently the subject categories are similar to Library of Congress terms, and (unlike most commercial Internet tools) the initial list produced by a search will include the information necessary to evaluate the relevancy and credibility of a site (e.g., author/creator, date, descriptor hyperlinks, ratings, and a brief summary or abstract of the information) **(see Figure 5.6)**. And, like an online library catalogue, you might need to broaden your search (i.e., search the broader concept or what your topic is about) to locate the distinctive subject categories that will lead you to pages about your topic.

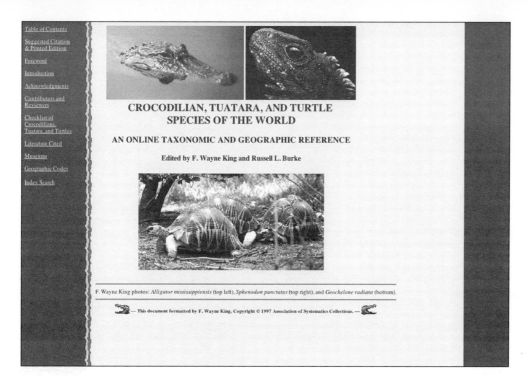

**CROCODILIAN, TUATARA, AND TURTLE
SPECIES OF THE WORLD**

AN ONLINE TAXONOMIC AND GEOGRAPHIC REFERENCE

Edited by F. Wayne King and Russell L. Burke

F. Wayne King photos: *Alligator mississippiensis* (top left), *Sphenodon punctatus* (top right), and *Geochelone radiata* (bottom).

— This document formatted by F. Wayne King. Copyright © 1997 Association of Systematics Collections. —

FIGURE 5.6

Web page property of the Florida Museum of Natural History
This excellent online resource (sources clearly documented) about reptiles was located by following related subject categories in the directory BUBL LINK 5:15. The category "Life Sciences" led to a page with more specialized terms, including "reptiles," which led to this annotated list of reptiles.

The following are some of the best subject guides currently available.

- *Librarians' Internet Index:* <www.lii.org>. **(See Figure 5.7.)** One of the earliest, most diligently maintained, and well-ordered subject guides on the Internet. It contains tens of thousands of quality sites that have been compiled by public librarians into 14 main topics and 300 subcategories. Its scope is limited, but it has been organized to facilitate the academic researcher with brief abstracts and related subject category links.

- *Infomine:* <http://infomine.ucr.edu>. Compiled and maintained by academic librarians from a number of distinguished universities and colleges (including the University of California, Wake Forest University, California State University, and the University of Detroit–Mercy), this subject guide contains more than 60,000 documents that are organized according to university-level subjects/disciplines.

FIGURE 5.7

This list of results for a search from "history AND Quebec" in the *Librarians' Internet Index* illustrates all of the benefits of a search guide: a small number of results (two), information about the author or creator of the site, the date the page was last updated, hyperlinks to related topics, and a brief abstract of the contents.

- *U.C. Berkeley & Internet Resources by Academic Discipline:* <http://sunsite2.berkeley.edu:8088/ERF/servlet/ERFmain?cmd=allSubjects>. Maintained by the University of California–Berkeley, this list of Internet resources on many academic disciplines has been selected by subject specialists.

- *Britannica's "Best of the Web":* <www.britannica.com>. Encyclopedia entries are available only to subscribers, but the "Best of the Web" category provides excellent summaries and reviews of web pages chosen by *Britannica* editors.

- *BUBL Information Service:* <http://bubl.ac.uk>. Funded by the United Kingdom, this very selective collection of Internet sources of mostly academic web resources is maintained by Strathclyde University in Scotland.

- *The Internet Public Library:* <www.ipl.org>. The "Reference Center" and "Subject Collections" are limited, but this collection, maintained by the University of Michigan School of Information, is an effort by volunteer librarians and librarian students to provide access to credible academic resources on the web.

- *About.com:* <www.about.com>. This subject guide can be uneven because each topic is overseen by a different "guide," who determines the content. Some areas are very good, whereas others are nonacademic in nature. However, with over a million documents catalogued, it deserves a try.

QUICK CHECK

Subject Directories and Search Engines Designed for Academic Use

Exceptional Subject Directories:

- Librarians' Internet Index: <www.lii.org>
- Infomine: <http://infomine.ucr.edu>
- U.C. Berkeley & Internet Resources by Academic Discipline: <http://sunsite2.berkeley.edu:8088/ERF/servlet/ERFmain?cmd=allSubjects>
- Britannica's Best of the Web: <www.britannica.com>
- BUBL LINK 5:15: <http://bubl.ac.uk>
- The Internet Public Library: <www.ipl.org>
- About.com: <www.about.com>

Effective Search Engines:

- AltaVista Advanced: <www.altavista.com/web/adv>
- Google: <www.google.com>
- Alltheweb Advanced: <www.alltheweb.com/advanced>

Learning Search Engine Features

Whether you are using a subject directory or a regular search engine, always take a few moments to familiarize yourself with its features. Make sure the tool recognizes phrase searching (i.e., the use of quotation marks around multiword phrases—"affirmative action"), uses Boolean terms, or has an advanced search mode that enables you to use these methods.

Using the Best Commercial Search Engines

It is best to begin with the subject guides described above because they are designed with research in mind and you can be confident that the web pages you find catalogued in them will be credible. Still, although they are reliable tools, they are not comprehensive. Certainly, for some topics (such as ecological threats to the rain forests or critical interpretations of *Moby Dick*) you will find a number of relevant sources. But for topics that are more regional in interest (such as local school bus regulations) or nonacademic in nature (such as wait-staff tipping protocol), you may have difficulty using these directories to locate the information you need.

In the latter case, or to locate additional web pages on your topic that were not catalogued in the academic subject guides that have just been discussed, you will need to use a search engine. Keep in mind, though, that not all search engines are created equal. Those that are best for shopping or travel (such as *Yahoo!*) are not usually the best for academic research. Here are some of the best search engines currently available for academic research, including some tips on how to use them effectively.

- *AltaVista Advanced:* <www.altavista.com/web/adv>. Perhaps one of the best search engines (because it is so large) for searching for distinctive exact terms or Boolean phrases, *AltaVista* searches the complete text of documents. You must use the "advanced search" feature for Boolean searches; the "sort by" feature makes large lists of returns more manageable.

- *Google:* <www.google.com>. One of the biggest search engines, *Google* employs a unique method of ranking results based on page popularity. A site is given high ranking if a lot of other web pages link to it. Sometimes this democratic approach really does result in locating the "best" pages (for instance, when shopping on the Internet), but it doesn't always ensure academic reliability. You will get the best results with *Google* if your search phrase is distinctive and technical.

- *Alltheweb Advanced:* <www.alltheweb.com/advanced>. Another large search engine, *Alltheweb's* advanced search feature allows you to conduct a variation on Boolean

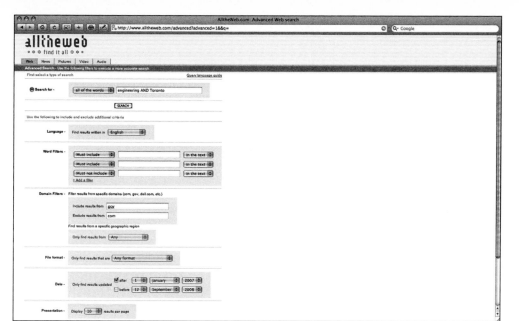

FIGURE 5.8

This search, using an
Advanced Search, will search
for websites that end with the
top-level domain "gov" and
exclude those with "com."

searches ("must include" = AND, "must not include" = NOT) and limit returns or hits according to domain (indicated by the last terms in the URL government [gov], education [edu], nonprofit organization [org], commercial [com], etc.) (see Figure 5.8).

You may have used a metasearch engine (such as *Dogpile, Metafind, Mamma, Clusty,* or *MetaCrawler*) in the past. As the name suggests, a metasearch engine simultaneously searches many search engines to provide a collective list of results. Although this sounds like a time-saver, there are a number of problems with this approach. First, many of the metasearch engines do not include *Google*. Second, most metasearch engines ignore quotation marks around multiword phrases and don't recognize Boolean search terms. Finally, none of the metasearch engines have advanced features that enable you to refine your search as you can with *Altavista* and *Alltheweb*.

Using Advanced Search Engine Features on the WWW

All of the search engines on the following page (except *Google*) have advanced search features. In the long run, you will save a great deal of time if you take a few minutes to learn how to use these features to limit your searches. A Boolean phrase in a standard search in most engines is interpreted as a "fuzzy AND" (which means that returns may have just one or both terms included). Most of the advanced search tools permit you to conduct a genuine Boolean search. In addition, these advanced features allow you to specify desired domains (the three letters of the URL that indicate the host address). Because many commercial and personal sites are biased or less credible, specifying domains that are government (gov), educational (edu), or nonprofit (org) can limit your results to more reliable websites. Advanced searches can also allow you to limit your results to web pages that have been updated in the last months or year, thus eliminating stale pages that might be out of date. Some even allow you to filter out inappropriate sites that might give false returns because words have been embedded in the page formatting.

Criteria for Evaluating Information Gathered from WWW Search Engines

When you locate a web page that is pertinent to your topic, you will need to evaluate the information carefully, using the criteria described more fully in Chapter 3 (purpose, reputation, intended audience, reliability, and timeliness). Because the WWW is not regulated like a library, the Internet researcher must assume even greater responsibility for conducting background checks to verify that the information on a web page is correct, credible, and properly documented. As always, the careful researcher is suspicious and never accepts information at face value. In addition to the tips on evaluation given in Chapter 3, asking the following questions about a website will help you determine its reliability.

What Is Its Purpose?

Although the Internet was originally developed primarily to distribute information for military purposes, its most common use today is e-commerce. It has created a revolution in how goods are advertised, bought, and sold. Because so much on the WWW is intended to persuade you to buy something, it is especially important to evaluate the purpose of a website before including the information it contains in your research project. For example, you might think an article entitled "The Benefits of Ritalin" offers an objective analysis of how this drug has helped to treat children with attention deficit hyperactivity disorder (ADHD). However, if it appears on the website of the pharmaceutical company that produces the drug, the purpose of the information is to sell the product. Even if a commercial web page contains accurate information, its undeniable bias makes it of questionable use in a scholarly project.

Where Does It Come From?

Because anyone can publish information on the WWW, determining the source of the information on a web page is especially important. Library sources prominently feature information about publishers and authors; however, on the Internet, authorship and organizational affiliation can be missing, misleading, or difficult to determine.

Be cautious about using an anonymous website in an academic research project. Remember that the source of the information you use determines its reliability, so anonymity will make your information suspect. If you know the name of the organization or author but have been unable to obtain any additional information, use the search engines *Google* or *AltaVista* and conduct a keyword search with the name enclosed in quotation marks. You might also see if an individual is listed at <www.whoswho-online.com> or a site called "Whois" at <www.whois.net>.

It is often difficult to determine the author or organization responsible for a website. Be sure not to confuse the "webmaster" with the author—a webmaster may not create the text contained on a page. Look for the following to locate the name of an organization or an author:

- A header, footer, or page watermark that announces the name of an organization.

- The name of an organization or institution in the URL (this may indicate an official affiliation, but it may not). For instance, a tilde (~) before a name usually indicates a personal site linked to an institutional server. This is not an official page.

- A hyperlink at the bottom, top, or left side of the page to the "home page" (sometimes the link will be labelled "About us"), or a hyperlink at bottom of the page to the author's home page.

- A link that allows you to e-mail the organization, the author, or the site webmaster (you can ask him/her about any affiliations).

You can also try "backtracking" through the URL by systematically deleting each "layer" or section of the address located between slashes. This might lead you back to the home page.

On the other hand, websites that have been produced by known and respected organizations (whether educational, governmental, or nonprofit) will make excellent sources. In addition, articles in online journals that use peer review by editors or web pages with articles that have been digitally reprinted from books or journals give evidence of being reliable and truthful.

Who Is the Typical Audience for the Information?

When used to support academic research, a source must be more than accurate: The subject must be investigated at a level of complexity appropriate for a post-secondary-level assignment. Much information on the Internet is designed for a general, rather than academic, audience. This is because the Internet has become a ready-reference tool for many people. Like the information in an encyclopedia or other general reference, web pages often provide succinct summaries and will be too basic to use as references for a college- or university-level paper. Your professor undoubtedly will require that you go beyond encyclopedia entries in your search for information. This is why I recommend using a subject guide rather than a commercial search engine—it will direct you to pages that are scholarly as well as accurate.

Always compare the information you locate on the web with what you have found using library tools (the online catalogue or full-text databases). Because the Internet is largely unregulated, web authors are sometimes careless about acknowledging sources. But like the information found in books in your school library or in articles in scholarly journals, a website source can be well researched and documented. Be especially cautious if a site offers numbers or statistics without identifying any sources. An absence of documentation suggests sloppiness, distortion, or worse. One sure indicator of a valid academic resource—on the web as in your own work—is thorough documentation.

When Was It Produced?

Just as it is often hard to locate the name of the sponsoring organization or author of a web page, it can sometimes be difficult to determine the date it was created or updated. For many research projects, it is essential that information be up to date in order to be accurate. As noted previously, knowledge undergoes constant revision, and you want your research to be based on the best information available at the moment. So it is important to note when information was created and determine whether it is still relevant. To determine the last update, enter the following: <javascript:alert(document.lastModified)> in the address field and then press "Enter." The last update information will appear in a window. Be cautious about using information from a web page that doesn't display a date or bears an old date, especially if it presents information that can change rapidly.

What Does It Look Like?

You can often evaluate a web page by paying attention to the tone, style, or proficiency of the writing. For instance, a pattern of grammatical errors and spelling mistakes is a dead giveaway that a careful, reliable author has not produced the material. Most scholars carefully check their work for these kinds of errors. An occasional mistake in punctuation or spelling is to be expected, but consistent writing errors should raise an alarm.

What Do Others Say About It?

Subject guides often offer brief synopses and reliability ratings. Like the abstracts included in most library resources, these give the researcher a quick impression of the relevancy and validity of a source. Also, confirmation by other sources is important in academic research. Even for topics that are heavily disputed, if an argument is sound, there will be other learned people who agree with it. Beware of radical opinions or ideas that are not substantiated in other places. If you cannot find corroboration, then you should exercise caution in using that information.

To sum up, then, the Internet has made innumerable sources available, but they vary in accuracy, reliability, and value. Train yourself to recognize a noteworthy resource by familiarizing yourself first with all your library offers on your topic. Then, when you are confident that you know enough to screen out information that is unreliable, unsupported, or poorly argued, venture out into the virtual world of the WWW. Researchers living in the digital age should never settle for unreliable information.

QUICK CHECK

Evaluate, Evaluate, Evaluate

Academic research on the Internet requires mastery in evaluating the credibility of sources. You must carefully appraise the web page to determine its purpose: Sarcasm and exaggeration reveal a biased opinion. Does the document present a well-reasoned, balanced approach to the topic?

- **Source:** Anonymity destroys credibility. Who is the document written by, and is it affiliated with a reliable organization?
- **Intended Audience:** Much on the Internet is designed for general consumption. Does the document acknowledge other sources and treat the topic with a certain amount of complexity?
- **Date of Publication:** Good research requires up-to-date information. Has the page been updated regularly?
- **Appearance:** You can tell something about a book by its cover. Is the website well written and grammatically correct, and does the general layout of the page (graphics, design, etc.) appear scholarly?
- **Reputation:** Nothing speaks louder than a good referral. Has the website received good reviews or been recommended in a summary or abstract?

EXERCISES

1. Since September 11, 2001, there has been a great deal posted on the Internet about terrorism. To get an idea of just how much, go to the *Google* search engine (<www.google.com>) and enter the search term "terrorism." Note the number of hits you get. Next, go to the *Librarians' Internet Index* (<www.lii.org>), and record the number of returns you get using the same search term ("terrorism"). Write a brief analysis that compares and contrasts these two search experiences.

 2. Besides supplying information that is of publishable quality, databases also provide suggestions for additional search terms/phrases or ways to refine previous search attempts that you won't find in most web search tools. If you are using the InfoTrac College Edition database in your course, use the passcode provided with this text to access the database and conduct a "Subject Guide" search using the term "terrorism." Review the InfoTrac College Edition subjects that contain the word *terrorism* and

choose three of the phrases that seem particularly interesting or relevant to you. Then access the search engine *Google* <www.google.ca> and perform searches using these search phrases. In a brief paragraph, compare and contrast the results from these searches with the outcome of the *Google* search you conducted in Exercise 1.

3. The following sites discuss the controversial issue of racial profiling:

   - <www.domelights.com/racprof1.htm>
   - <www.ocasi.org/index.php?catid=117>
   - <www.cbc.ca/news/background/racial_profiling/>
   - <www.racialprofilinganalysis.neu.edu>

   Write a brief evaluation (using the criteria presented in this chapter and in Chapter 3) analyzing why these websites would/would not be credible sources of information for a post-secondary-level research paper on this topic.

 4. Now conduct a "Keyword" search in the InfoTrac College Edition database using the search phrase "racial profiling AND terrorism." Choose one of the results from this list and write a paragraph in which you compare/contrast the reliability and credibility of this source to the four websites in Exercise 3.

6

Field Research Online

"You can tell whether a man is clever by his answers. You can tell whether a man is wise by his questions."

MAHFOUZ NAGUIB

Thus far, we have focused on research of "secondary" sources—information generated, and then published, by other researchers. For most topics, this is your most likely source for information to complete your research paper. At times, though, you may need to carry out "primary" research—original information generated by you. In this chapter, we are going to discuss two methods for collecting original data on your subject: **interviews** and **surveys**.

When you interview or survey people to obtain their opinions, you are conducting fieldwork. Just as the value of any written source must be evaluated according to specific criteria (i.e., whether the source is up to date, pertinent, credible, and reasonably unbiased), so, too, is the value of fieldwork tied to how careful you are in choosing whom and how to query.

Research Ethics

Before considering how to conduct research, we need to briefly discuss research ethics. Research ethics concerns the rights, health, safety, and privacy of the research subjects (the people that your research examines). As a researcher, you must adhere to the rules for conducting ethical research. Each college and university has its own research ethics guidelines, and you should consult with your professor. However, these are some of the most common research situations to consider:

- The research involves human subjects
- The research uses human data or human material
- There are serious health and safety implications

- Animal experiments are involved
- There is a risk of damage to the health of the environment
- The impact of the research process or results may be emotionally damaging
- The research is politically or socially sensitive
- The source of funding for the research has the potential to compromise the university's position as a publicly funded charitable body

Although it is unlikely that your research will pose any ethical problems for your research subjects or your institution, you should talk through any concerns you may have with your professor prior to starting.

Research Interviews

The Value of Interviews

Conducting an interview with an expert on a subject can dramatically enhance the quality of your research project. Speaking to someone who has had firsthand or extensive experience with your topic is exciting. And that excitement will often infuse your writing, making it more interesting for the reader as well. Of course, interviews alone can never replace the other forms of research we have already discussed in the first five chapters of this book. Don't assume that an expert will do your research for you or that speaking with an expert will substitute for thorough research. You will still need to conduct library research using the online catalogue, databases, and select subject guides on the Internet. An interview is simply one more source of information.

Identifying Interviewees

The first question to consider when planning an interview is "Who?" You likely have access to more experts than you might first imagine. As a student at a college or university, for example, you have immediate access to experts in a wide range of fields. My former student who researched the turtle/salmonella law was able to interview a biology professor who had special training in herpetology and a nursing instructor who gave her firsthand information about the medical treatment of salmonella infection. As a citizen, you have access to local, and perhaps even national, government officials. Another student who was investigating the county school and bus scheduling system was able to interview a trustee of the local school board. And as a member of the virtual community made possible by the World Wide Web, you have access to countless experts worldwide. A former student interested in the inequities of the financial aid system for nontraditional students was able to e-mail a government official with questions about student loan policies and received answers to his questions within a few days. The Internet gives you immediate access to innumerable experts who can provide vital, direct information about your subject—or point you in the direction of those who can.

If you're lucky, you might already have an expert in mind whom you would like to interview, but most times you will need to find someone who is an authority on your topic. One obvious source is the telephone book or an online telephone directory. Are you investigating the practices of day care providers? Consider contacting local day care centres. Are you examining stalking laws? Check an online "800" number phone book <www.inter800.com> for the toll-free telephone numbers of specific associations that assist victims of domestic violence or sexual harassment. You might feel apprehensive about calling someone you don't know for an interview, but most people welcome the opportunity to discuss their work, either in person, by phone, or by e-mail. It's a good idea to suggest these different options, because some people are more comfortable with e-mail or find it easier to fit an e-mail interview into their schedule. Be sure to call for an interview a few weeks in advance. Before you call, write out exactly why you want to speak to the person and what information you hope to obtain. Be as specific as you can about your research project, and be prepared to explain or give further details if necessary. If you sound knowledgeable and focused, the person you call will be more likely to agree to an interview.

Don't overlook the possibility of tracking down experts through the Internet. Many organizations have web pages with links that allow you to e-mail questions. If during the course of your research you locate an especially pertinent or noteworthy source published on the Internet, and an e-mail address is provided, then contact the author **(see Figure 6.1)**. Make sure that your questions extend beyond the information provided on the web page. You'll also want to allow enough time for a thoughtful reply; you might check your e-mail many times a day, but you can't expect everyone to respond so quickly.

FIGURE 6.1

This detail-rich website is a tremendous resource for information on education in Ontario: it contains up-to-date information and covers education from grade school through college and university, looks at popular topics and employment, and provides current education news and links.

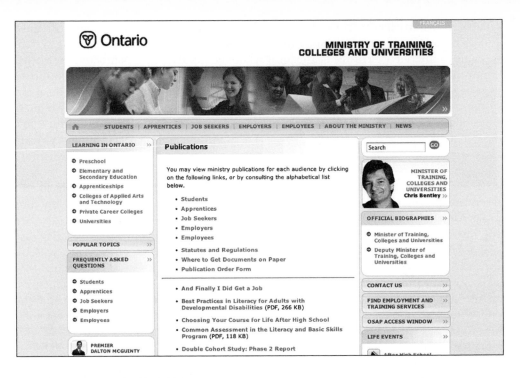

QUICK CHECK

Strategies for Locating an Expert

- *Consider your campus first:* Professors at your college or university are an excellent source of information, and they are usually willing to be interviewed for school projects.

- *Approach local officials and agencies:* Part of being a public servant is answering the public's questions. For example, government officials, police, fire, school, and hospital administrators (among others) in your community will often agree to meet with you.

- *Search the phone book:* Many organizations have toll-free numbers. Explore <www.inter800.com> for contact numbers of experts on your topic.

- *E-mail a noted expert:* Have you found a website with excellent information? See if there is a link that allows you to e-mail your questions to the author.

Conducting Interviews

Interviews can be conducted face-to-face, by phone, or by e-mail. For undergraduate research projects, e-mail is often an excellent means of carrying out an interview. In fact, even if the authority you are consulting is located on your campus or in your town, you might want to consider conducting the interview via e-mail. There are a number of advantages to this approach. Sometimes it is difficult to coordinate schedules to meet face-to-face; by using e-mail to send your questions and responses, you can avoid this inconvenience. Moreover, by receiving questions in writing in advance, your expert can provide more thoughtful responses. Finally, because you will receive your answers in writing, you will be less likely to forget information or misquote your expert.

Preparing Your Interview Questions

Once you have located an expert you would like to interview, take the time to develop good questions. Many novice researchers mistakenly think that once they locate an authority and set up an interview, the hard part is over, but composing thoughtful questions—questions that will elicit interesting responses—is equally demanding. In fact, preparing for an interview is an excellent way to refocus your project because it forces you to rethink the questions with which you began your research.

Avoid general questions that will elicit vague answers. Instead, do your homework. Read up on the topic (and the person you'll be interviewing, if possible) so that you can focus your questions and provide an opportunity for the expert you are interviewing to discuss his or her full range of knowledge. Ask for information that is not readily available from other sources. For instance, the student interested in reptiles asked her biology instructor what steps herpetologists took to protect themselves from exposure to the salmonella bacteria and whether he thought reptiles should be kept as pets. In her interview with a nursing instructor, she asked about the specifics of treating salmonella—what kinds of symptoms the patients suffered, how long the illness normally lasts, and what the therapy was like. She also asked if the nursing instructor would allow her own children to keep a pet reptile, given the danger of infection.

Here are some additional suggestions to help you prepare for the interview:

- Prepare your questions in writing. Doing so will enable you to get the exact phrasing you want and arrange the questions in a logical order.

- Limit your questions to a few that are very specific. It is better to ask three or four pointed questions than eight ambiguous ones. This is especially true in e-mail interviews. Because your expert needs to type his or her replies, you are more likely to get thorough answers if you keep your questions to a minimum.

- Avoid questions that can be answered with a simple "yes" or "no." Instead, ask *who, what, when, where,* and—most important—*how* and *why* questions.

- Develop questions that are primarily interpretive or evaluative (e.g., "What is the biggest danger the salmonella bacteria pose to a patient?"); they will elicit the most useful and interesting responses.

- Consider ending the interview with a question that leads to new information. For example, you might ask your expert to recommend other people to interview or specific books or articles to read.

Mastering the Logistics of Face-to-Face Interviews

If you are conducting the interview face-to-face, it is important that you keep an accurate record of all answers. No one likes to be misquoted. In fact, because I have been misquoted so frequently, I no longer give face-to-face interviews with our school newspaper staff unless they agree to let me review any quotations they plan to use before the article is published.

Here are some suggestions for conducting the interview:

- To ensure accuracy, consider tape-recording the interview. If you do, be sure to obtain permission from the person being interviewed in advance.

- Take notes—even if you record the interview. Tape recordings have been known to fail.

- Put quotation marks around any statements in your notes that are direct quotations. Check these with the person being interviewed to make sure you have quoted him or her correctly.

- Be flexible. Sometimes a question will generate a response that inspires a follow-up question that you haven't prepared beforehand. If that happens, don't hesitate to add questions or let the interview take a slightly different direction.

- Before you end the interview, check your notes for accuracy. If (in the course of your conversation) your expert furnished you with explicit details or statistics, confirm them while you're still with the person.

- Immediately following the interview, jot down your impressions and complete any unfinished statements in your notes. Clearly mark information that might be most useful to your project.

- If you need to clarify a point or a quotation, make sure you contact the interviewee. To be courteous, you should follow up the interview by sending a short thank you to the person you interviewed.

TIP

» **Using Online Discussions as Sources**

You might be tempted to use a listserv (sometimes called a mailing group or discussion list) or newsgroup (often referred to as a discussion group) to gather personal opinions and ideas about your topic. There are, however, limitations to the usefulness of these forums. The discussions can be an excellent catalyst for stimulating your thinking, but many contributors do not use their real names; the anonymity that surrounds most of the participants makes this an ineffective means of gathering authoritative information. Secondly, many of the people participating in these online groups are interested novices, like yourself, rather than experts, and it is difficult to guarantee the credibility of anyone you meet online.

Surveys

Surveys are statistical studies of sample populations that seek to understand specific aspects of people's lives, such as views on political parties or buying preferences. If you have ever taken a statistics or methods course in psychology or sociology, you know that there is a science to surveys. Unless you take time to learn the rules about how to compile an accurate sample; unless you compose forthright, revealing questions; and unless you correctly interpret the results, you cannot expect your fieldwork to fulfill the strict specifications of academic research. Confirm with your instructor to determine the appropriateness of surveys for your research project.

Composing an Effective Survey

Composing a survey is very different from conducting an interview. Interview questions are like essay questions—they are open-ended and attempt to draw out extended answers. A survey, however, is more like an objective test—the questions should elicit short, yet revealing, responses.

Examples of Good Survey Questions

- Does the college need to provide more student parking? Yes–No
- Should talk shows that deal with controversial, adult subjects be aired only after 9 P.M.? Yes–No
- How often do you read local newspapers? Daily. 2–3 times per week. Weekly. Less than once per week.

The questions should be phrased so people can answer quickly, and the responses must fit a pattern that enables results to be easily compiled and compared. Most questions should be answered as simply as "yes or no," "true or false," or with a ranking scale—say, from 1 to 5.

Developing a high-quality survey requires that you already have a strong grasp of the subject you are studying. You should have already completed a good deal of research and be familiar with the most significant ideas related to your topic. This will enable you to design questions that elicit relevant and insightful responses to your questions. You also need to understand the purpose of the survey: what do you really want to learn from the responses you gather? Before implementing the survey, ask yourself whether the questions you've designed will generate the information you need.

Here are some general guidelines for preparing your survey questions:

- Ask no more than 8 to 10 questions.
- Use clear, concise, and unambiguous language. (Test your questions on friends, and simplify any phrasing they find unclear or confusing.)
- Phrase your questions so they can be answered with a "yes or no" or "true or false" response or a range of alternative choices (i.e., strongly disagree, disagree, no opinion, agree, strongly agree). Maintain consistent response options to avoid confusing your participant.
- A survey question may gather factual information or ask for opinion. In either case, make sure the question doesn't encourage the respondent to give a particular response.

An example of a "leading" question: Are you dissatisfied with the administration's failure to solve the parking problem on campus?

Revised: Do you think the administration has responded appropriately to the parking problem on campus?

- Arrange your questions from easiest to hardest. This allows your respondents a chance to warm up before being asked the most challenging queries.

- Prepare your surveys so they are easy to read and complete. Instructions should be brief and explicit. Limit the amount of writing required—instead, respondents should be able to circle or check responses. (This tactic will increase the percentage of fully completed surveys.)

- Don't ask for unnecessary or revealing personal information. The more anonymous the survey is, the more likely you will receive an honest response. (If a person's name, age, sex, religious affiliation, employment status, or race isn't relevant, don't ask. If you need personal information to properly interpret the results, then promise confidentiality and honour your pledge.) If you need to capture personal information of this type, check with your institution for guidelines on how to conduct research of this kind.

Administering the Survey

Like an interview, whom you ask to answer your questionnaire is important. For example, if you want to know what parents think about an issue, then you need to distribute the survey to people with children. Therefore, you will need to consider how to best identify and reach representative members of your targeted group. Your objective is to create a "random" sampling. A simple random sample ensures that every possible sample has an equal chance of being selected from the population. This allows you, the researcher, to interpret the results from your sample as representative of the larger population without surveying each and every person in the larger population.

Failure to identify your target group accurately or to distribute the survey to them effectively will skew your results. For example, I once served on a committee that met with student government officers to determine students' most pressing concerns for change on campus. They had surveyed a few hundred students, who were asked to rank how important certain changes in student services or school policies were to them. Expanding the parking lots, improving the food service, and bringing better entertainment to campus ranked very high. But I was surprised to see that providing childcare assistance was ranked last, since a large percentage of the students in my classes are single mothers who are struggling to balance parenting with their education. When I asked how the survey had been administered, I realized why the results were so curious. No effort had been made to poll men and women in equal numbers, and most of the surveys had been distributed at school functions (such as athletic and social events) that a busy student/mom would most likely not attend. It was clear to me that the results didn't accurately depict the concerns of our student body because the sampling didn't represent the diversity of our student population.

You should model your methods of survey on the professional model—have a random and broad spectrum of respondents.

Here are some general suggestions to help guide you in administering your survey:

- Administer the survey yourself to allow you to describe accurately how the survey was conducted.

- Give yourself ample time to administer the survey and tabulate and interpret the results.

- Keep the number of the sample realistic. You might think that the more questionnaires completed, the better. In reality, you often get an effective outcome from a fairly small number of results, as long as the sampling is random.

- Use a standardized form to keep track of answers. (You might choose to administer the survey orally, but you should develop a standard answer sheet on which to record responses.)

- Record when, where, and how your survey was conducted.

- Carefully tabulate your results.

Conducting Surveys by E-mail

Surveys, like personal interviews, can be conducted effectively via e-mail. Abide by the same rules concerning random sampling (don't just e-mail the survey to your friends or family—you must try for a cross-sampling of opinion). Make sure that you specify a date of completion, and be prepared to remind people to return them to you on time.

Reporting Your Research Methods

When you report your results in your essay, present your findings in a manner that will make sense to your readers (i.e., use percentages or ratios). Always describe the methods you used to collect the information and how you selected your survey participants. Indicate the date(s) on which you conducted the survey, where you questioned people, and the procedures you followed. Most importantly, specify the limits of your study. Note the number of people questioned, the general population they represented, and the techniques you used to ensure that this was a random sample.

Personally interviewing an authority on your subject or conducting a survey of opinions on your topic can be a useful research experience. Because people are such a great source of information, these methods can reveal ideas and attitudes not available from other sources. Nevertheless, be careful to qualify any conclusions you draw from these data, and resist overstating the results.

EXERCISES

1. Your psychology teacher has assigned a research paper project, and you have chosen to write about eating disorders. Compose a list of potential experts (using the suggestions you received in this chapter) whom you might interview to help complete this assignment.

2. If you are using InfoTrac College Edition in your course, access the following article in the database [*Hint:* conduct a "Title Search"]:

   Browne, Lorna, and Anthony Curtis. "Eat to live or love to eat? The paradox of eating disorders." Psychology Review 7.4 *(2001): 20–25.*

   Using the information contained in this article (and keeping in mind the suggestions made in this chapter), compose a list of five questions you could ask in an interview with one of the experts you identified in Exercise 1.

3. You decide to prepare a survey of the students at your school about eating disorders. Briefly describe in one paragraph what your target group would be and how you would administer the survey to ensure a random sampling of that group.

4. Access the following article in the InfoTrac College Edition database [*Hint:* conduct a "Title Search"]:

   Kowalski, Kathiann M. "Body image: how do you see yourself? How you feel about your body has a big impact on your health. Learn to like the person you see in the mirror!" Current Health 2 *29.7 (2003): 29–35.*

   Using the information contained in this article (and keeping in mind the suggestions made in this chapter), compose a list of five survey questions you could ask of the group you identified in Exercise 3.

PART
3

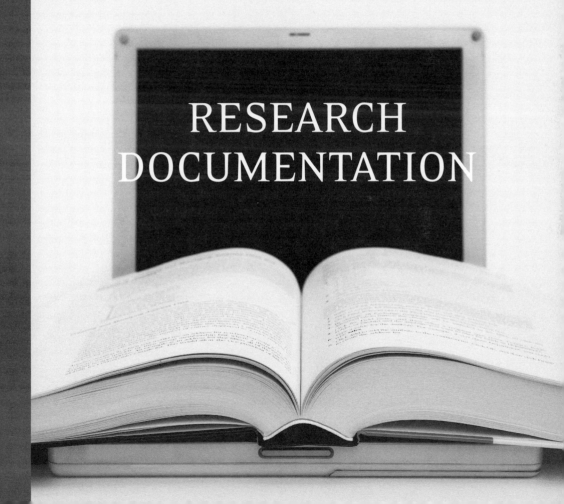

RESEARCH
DOCUMENTATION

7 Documentation: General Rules

"The wisdom of the wise and the experience of the ages are perpetuated by quotations."

BENJAMIN DISRAELI

If you are like many people, you wait until you've written your paper before composing a Works Cited page. For many, this step is an afterthought. But the Works Cited page—where you document the sources you have drawn from to conduct your research—is actually the foundation upon which a research essay sits. Many professors turn to the Works Cited page first, even before they read an essay, to obtain a general impression of the research that underpins the paper. (In fact, I know several professors who will refuse to grade a paper if there are too many errors on the Works Cited page.) Indeed, a research paper is only as good as its sources. If you think about that for a moment, you'll see that it makes sense. After all, what is a reasonable person going to trust more: an argument based on the best available evidence or one grounded in outdated, obscure, or unreliable information? Moreover, if you haven't accurately formatted this documentation page, it will betray (at best) that you are unfamiliar with academic "protocol" or (at worst) that you don't care about the quality of your work. And if *you* don't care, why should your reader?

Properly documenting a research paper requires that you pay meticulous attention to detail. It requires that you accurately identify the nature of your source and that you distinguish and follow the proper format for citing that source, both in the text and on the Works Cited page.

In a preelectronic library, it was fairly easy to determine the type of source with which you were working. The most common were books, articles in periodicals, articles in reference works (i.e., dictionaries or encyclopedias), government documents, pamphlets, or interviews. With the advent of computers, and then the Internet, new systems of delivery have made this task of identification more complex and varied. Now information might also be delivered by a CD-ROM, a library database, a website, an online subscription service, a podcast, or an e-mail. What makes documentation even more complicated is that, as technology changes, these forms are continuously morphing into new modes of data transmission. This makes it extremely challenging for even the most careful writer to remain up to date on the conventions of documentation.

Nevertheless, because improper documentation can sometimes mean the difference between a grade of A or B, it is in your best interest to incorporate source material into your research paper correctly. You will make a strong impression, either positive or negative, by how carefully you integrate material into your essay, acknowledge your research within the text of the paper, and document your resources on the Works Cited page.

A Few Words About Plagiarism: *DON'T DO IT!*

Many college and university students are understandably uncertain about what constitutes plagiarism. The student's confusion stems from a number of factors. For one thing, beginning writers often aren't taught to paraphrase properly and/or to acknowledge sources when they begin writing "research" papers in elementary school. Thus, very early on they develop the bad habit of plagiarizing throughout their academic careers—often without fully realizing it. For another thing, the "cut and paste" nature of the Internet has blurred the boundaries of intellectual property; of what must be formally cited. But don't be deceived—your professors expect you to respect the ideas and words of others and to properly document any use you make of them.

Plagiarizers Are Not Born; They're Made

I remember when I wrote my first researched essay—it was on Texas. I consulted the *Encyclopedia Britannica,* carefully copied, word for word, pertinent information from this reference work, and then skillfully wove in some of my own words and phrases. Occasionally I enclosed significant sentences in quotation marks, but there were many directly quoted words and phrases that I did not indicate as such, and much of the rest of the essay was a thinly disguised facsimile of the encyclopedia article that I (incorrectly) considered a "paraphrase." I made a cover out of construction paper, crayoned a likeness of the Lone Star State on the front, and tied the report together with a piece of brightly coloured yarn. When I handed it in to my fourth grade teacher, she praised my efforts and rewarded me with an A+. Many students begin their careers as plagiarizers in just this way.

By the time they reach high school, they have become more ingenious. Instead of relying on an encyclopedia alone, they use a variety of sources. They learn to create Works Cited pages or bibliographies (although they might not follow a specific format for this). They piece together sentences from various sources, change a phrase here and there, and skillfully disguise thoughts and phrases that are not their own. In order to better conceal their theft, some especially clever students might even borrow heavily from a "secret" source that they don't acknowledge in their bibliography or Works Cited page. I have known a number of students who have become very adept at making these plagiarized reports look like their own writing; in actuality, these papers are what I call "plagiarism quilts"—other people's words and ideas stitched together, more or less seamlessly.

The Truth About Plagiarism

Even if you haven't developed such bad habits, you might still be confused about what constitutes plagiarism. This confusion is exacerbated by the way images and content are often "borrowed" on the Internet without proper attribution. When surfing the web, you have probably encountered identical images or articles on different pages. This phenomenon stems from the fact that it is very easy to "cut and paste" graphics or text from the web. All of this might lead you to conclude that the Internet is a big "grab bag" from which you can freely take what you want. However, this is *not* true.

There is a great deal of misinformation about this subject circulating in the halls of academe. I have had students confidently assert that as long as they change at least 10 percent of the words in a sentence, it is no longer considered a direct quote, and there is no need to use quotation marks or document the source. Others believe that they need to attribute a direct quote to a source, but a paraphrase doesn't need to be acknowledged. Sometimes I have received papers with little or no direct quotation, but after every sentence there is a parenthetical citation. This is a sad attempt at making a "plagiarism quilt" legitimate. However—and this is the important point—in spite of the students' efforts at documentation, *these aren't really research papers.* They are the subtly altered words and ideas of others represented as original creations. Too many students define plagiarism only as copying a friend's term paper or downloading a paper off the Internet and submitting it, in total, as their own. The truth is, plagiarism takes many forms.

Schools Get Tough on Plagiarizers

The Internet has made it easier for students to plagiarize. There are millions of legitimate documents that can be copied, as well as "paper mills" that offer thousands of essays (both free and for sale). At times the temptation to "borrow" writing or ideas and represent them as your own might seem overwhelming. After all, a lot of students are doing it. Statistics indicate that instances of academic dishonesty are on the rise. However, the web has also made it easier for professors to recognize plagiarism. Many schools are fighting back and enforcing tough policies to ensure that students do their own work, as well as subscribing to plagiarism detection programs such as Turnitin.com. Turnitin works by comparing the words and sentences in your essay with hundreds of thousands of other essays on the Internet or previously processed by Turnitin. Tools like Turnitin have increased the ease and accuracy with which professors can identify incidences of plagiarism. Resist the urge to take these types of shortcuts. The consequences can be severe.

The Many Faces of Plagiarism

Plagiarism can be either intentional or accidental. Whether students intentionally set out to deceive a professor and pass off someone else's words and ideas as their own, carelessly fail to place quotation marks around another writer's words, or neglect to place the proper citation at the end of a paraphrase, the end result is the same. *All of these examples constitute plagiarism*—it's just that some are more egregious than others.

- **Deliberate plagiarism** involves copying someone else's words and/or ideas and passing them off as your own. (This could be an entire paper, portions of a paper, or simply copying the language and sentence patterns of another person's work.)

- **Accidental plagiarism** involves failing to place quotation marks around another writer's words (even if you provide a source at the end of your essay) and failing to provide the proper citation when you rely on another person's ideas.

The important thing to remember is that *whenever* you incorporate information from someone else's work into your own writing, regardless of whether it is a direct quote, a careful paraphrase, or a brief summary, *you must properly indicate the source.* The one exception to this rule is information that legitimately could be considered **common knowledge**. Common knowledge is information that most readers are familiar with or could be easily found from widely available sources. For example, the date of Confederation (July 1, 1867) or the capital of Alberta (Edmonton) are all examples of common knowledge. In cases such as these, you need not indicate the source of the information.

What constitutes common knowledge varies by audience (i.e., who is reading your research paper). That is, what is considered common knowledge will be dependent on who is reading your research paper. (Age, profession, and level of education are all variables that can affect your decision to document a fact or not.) Most professors would agree that if you can find the information undocumented in several different sources, it is probably common knowledge. (Be careful, though; the cut-and-paste nature of the web has resulted in incredible abuse of intellectual property. The judgment of web authors should not guide your own decision regarding what is common knowledge.) Most instructors would encourage you to err on the side of caution. In other words, if you are unsure whether something is common knowledge, it is better to go ahead and document it.

It is important to remember that if the information is the intellectual property of another writer—whether that information takes the form of statistical evidence, individual opinion, distinctive analysis, original inquiry, or especially compelling phrasing—you need to document the source. In such cases, you must always enclose exact words or unique phrasing in quotation marks and include a proper in-text citation as well as a corresponding entry on your Works Cited page. If you use the same ideas as your source—even if you paraphrase—then you must acknowledge the original in a parenthetical citation and on the Works Cited page. Your instructor expects that as a member of an academic community, you will respect and uphold these basic rules of academic integrity.

A Sure Way to Impress: Incorporate and Document Quotes with Skill

As I mentioned at the beginning of this chapter, how you handle research sources in your paper makes a powerful impact. The most significant reason for using direct quotations or paraphrasing is to provide support for your claims or add credibility to your writing. If you let this principle guide you, you will develop expertise as a writer. But it is not enough to avoid plagiarizing; if you want to incorporate information into your project effectively, you must manage your sources skillfully and accurately.

General Rules for Incorporating Direct Quotations

One error that betrays many novice writers is that their essays are too dependent on direct quotations. This error can be manifested in two ways, but both create the impression that the writer lacks confidence in his or her thinking or writing. The first mistake is to quote too often. When the bulk of an essay is the words of others, it seems as if the writer of the essay has "disappeared." The second is to allow quotations to make your points for you, rather than citing the words or ideas of others to support your own assertions and opinions. Your words and ideas should always dominate the essay. Here are some rules of thumb to help you avoid either error.

- **No more than 15 percent of your paper should be direct quotation.** Most of the writing should be your own. Use the words and opinions of others only to support your own points and ideas.

- **Keep quotations short.** Resist the temptation to quote long passages of text, even if it seems remarkable and strikingly worded. Instead, smoothly incorporate fragments of direct quotations into your own sentences, making certain that the sentence structure is correct and makes sense.

- **Clearly identify each quotation**. If the purpose of direct quotation is to lend credibility to your writing, then you should indicate the authority behind the words. Never simply plop quotations into your paper without specifying who is speaking. Instead, use a signal phrase (sometimes called an identifying tag) to set up the quotation properly.

- **Precede and follow quotations with your own commentary.** Don't use a direct quote to *make* your point. Instead, state your idea in your own words, and supplement that with a quotation from an expert.

- **Interweave your sources.** When quotations from the same source are all clustered in one portion of a paper, it can be a clear sign of a "plagiarism quilt." Instead, your paper should blend information from different sources to create your own analysis.

Example:

- *Original Source Material:*

    "Only by reducing can we turn the 'waste generation' into something more sustainable"

    From: "Wasted Breath" by David Murray in Canadian Geographic.

    "The best case scenario is that information about e-waste is not available in this province. The worst case scenario is that no such information or program exists. Either way, my computers end up in New Brunswick landfills, and I still don't know what to do with our used machine"

    From: "Wasted Breath" by J. Jensen in Canadian Geographic.

- *Improper Incorporation of Quotations:*

    Has recycling and reducing waste been successful? "The best case scenario is that information about e-waste is not available in this province. The worst case scenario is that no such information or program exists. Either way, my computers end up in New Brunswick landfills, and I still don't know what to do with our used machine" (Jensen 15–16).

NOTE: The use of a question, rather than a statement, to lead into the quoted information accentuates the tentativeness of the writer. Also, the quote is excessively long without a proper introduction into the subject matter (recycling). The quote is also a personal reflection and might not accurately reflect present reduction and recycling programs across Canada.

- ***Quotations Skillfully Incorporated:***

In a series of letters to the editor in the 2006 June edition of Canadian Geographic, *debating the effectiveness of reducing and recycling in Canada, one writer from Calgary, David Murray, states that the present generation must refuse to indulge in disposable items, thereby reducing waste and "turn the 'waste generation' into something more sustainable" (15). Another writer, based in New Brunswick, identifies the problem of not being provided with adequate information on the availability of recycling programs. She states: "either way, my computers end up in New Brunswick landfills, and I still don't know what to do with our used machine" (Jensen 15–16).*

NOTE: With a proper introduction into the subject matter, as well as by referencing the personal experiences and opinions of two authors from different geographic regions, a more accurate picture is developed on the efficacy of recycling and reducing across Canada. Further, the quotes are reduced in size and combined to provide an analysis.

General Rules for Paraphrasing

To paraphrase is to rewrite someone else's ideas in your own words. This is a simple concept, but it is extremely difficult to execute. The challenge of paraphrasing is to relate accurately the sense of a text without duplicating the language. Here are some suggestions to help you paraphrase correctly.

- **Write your paraphrase from memory.** It is very difficult to paraphrase without plagiarizing; if you attempt to rephrase something while you are looking at the original, you are almost doomed to failure. Instead, write your paraphrase without consulting the source. Afterward, compare it to the original and check for accuracy.

- **Indicate any direct quotation.** Any words or phrases that appear in the original source are considered direct quotes. You must enclose those words with quotation marks.

- **Clearly identify your source.** Just like a direct quote, a paraphrase needs to be introduced to indicate the authority of the source. In fact, an introductory, or signal, phrase is even more important because there are no quotation marks to distinguish these ideas from your own.

NOTE: Remember, whether it is a direct quote or a paraphrase, you must always indicate your source within the text and on a Works Cited page.

Example:

- *Original Source Material:*

  Some writers claim that the coming demographic change will not affect the costs of health-care very much, but their arguments mask the reorganization necessary. We have a health-care system that was designed when the median age of Canadians was 26; it is now 38.

  From: MacKnight et al. (2003). Response to the Romanow Report: The Canadian Geriatrics Society. Geriatrics Today: Journal of the Canadian Geriatrics Society, *2003 6(1), 11–15.*

- *Improper Paraphrase:*

  According to MacKnight and colleagues (2003) the argument by some writers that demographic changes will not affect the costs of health-care hides the reorganization that is necessary. The Canadian health-care system was originally designed for the average age of 26, but it is now 38.

NOTE: Even though MacKnight and colleagues are cited using correct format according to APA, the wording and structure is far too similar to the original source. This would be considered plagiarism.

- *Proper Paraphrase:*

  An article reviewing the Romanow Report on health-care in Canada suggests that some researchers are not considering the new demographic changes and that arguments put forward by these researchers hide "the reorganization necessary" (MacKnight et al., 2003, p. 12). MacKnight and colleagues further suggest that the original health-care system was devised when the average Canadian median age was 26. It is presently estimated that the average median age is now 38.

NOTE: The source is clearly identified in the paragraph, the main ideas are summarized in unique wording and sentence structure, and where exact wording from the original is used, it appears in quotation marks. The paraphrase includes the correct citation method according to the system chosen, in this case APA.

General Rules for Citing Sources

Any time you directly quote or paraphrase a source, you must provide the information necessary for a reader to locate easily that document and the specific information you have just cited. Students sometimes complain that the rules concerning documentation are too difficult and arbitrary. Indeed, for both the in-text and Works Cited page documentation, there are strict rules about what information to include, in what order it should be given, and how it is to be punctuated. Although many students seem baffled by these rules, the reason for this "pickiness" is to reduce confusion by having everyone conform to the same conventions. Documentation rules serve to establish a uniform, universal format so a reader can quickly determine what type of source is being cited and, if desired, track down the text.

T I P

> » **Format Citations and Develop Your Reference List as You Write**

Many students make the mistake of leaving the task of documentation until after a paper is completely written. Then they must go back and locate all of the places where they have cited information and retrieve the required details to correctly document the source. They may overlook places in their paper where they need to cite their sources, forget where a quotation came from, or misplace the source they used. It is much better to format as you write a paper. Include a parenthetical citation after any direct quotation or paraphrase. Word processing programs make it very easy to keep a current Works Cited page as you work. Even if you are not sure of the format, you can type (or copy and paste, if you are using electronic sources) the necessary information (author[s], editor[s], title, place of publication, publisher, date of publication, page numbers, date of access, etc.) on the last page or keep a separate file with this information.

What many students don't realize until late in their academic careers (sometimes not until graduate school) is that there is a logic to documenting essays. In some ways, their problem is similar to the difficulties many students have who study organic chemistry. I once asked a friend of mine who teaches that subject why so many seemingly capable students wash out when they take this course. He explained that the course requires students to memorize an enormous amount of seemingly disconnected information before they can discern a pattern. Few students are able to see the interrelatedness of what they are studying until they are well into the semester. With no conceptual grid to help them make sense of the myriad facts they are attempting to muster, many falter.

The rules for documenting sources can seem like that. When you look at a style handbook, it can appear that there is no rhyme or reason to formatting rules. However, there is method to the madness. The in-text citation directs a reader to the first piece of information listed in the entry on the Works Cited page. Normally, that is the author's last name. (If there is no author listed, then it will cue the reader to the next piece of information listed: the title of the work.)

There are two major styles of documentation: the MLA (Modern Language Association) style, which is commonly used in the humanities, and the APA (American Psychological Association) style, which is usually employed in the social sciences and some sciences, such as nursing. Although there are some significant differences between these formats, they are similar. Both require the following information.

1. A signal phrase
   - usually appears at the beginning of a quotation or paraphrase, but can appear mid-phrase
   - includes the name(s) of the author(s) or the title of the book, article, periodical, or website from which the information originates
   - can use a variety of "verbs of address," such as:

adds	compares	grants	refutes
admits	confirms	illustrates	rejects
agrees	contends	implies	reports
argues	declares	insists	responds
asserts	denies	notes	suggests
believes	disputes	observes	thinks
claims	emphasizes	points out	writes

2. A citation
   - provides a brief reference to the source document in the text of the essay
   - is located inside parentheses and appears in the same paragraph as the information it documents
   - normally appears at the end of the sentence that features the information being cited
   - may appear in midsentence, especially if information from more than one source appears in the same statement

3. A Works Cited reference
   - appears on a Works Cited page at the conclusion of the paper
   - includes all of the required bibliographic information

These three components (signal phrase, parenthetical citation, and Works Cited reference) work together; if you exclude one of them, you have compromised the accuracy of your documentation. If the purpose of direct quotation and paraphrase is to lend authority to your essay, then failing to identify the source seriously undercuts your efforts.

EXERCISES

1. Briefly (in two or three sentences), and in your own words, explain why it is important to include outside sources in a research paper. At some point in this paragraph, correctly incorporate any portion(s) of the text below as a direct quote. Follow the suggestions you received in this chapter to do this successfully.

   Use quotations selectively to add clarity, emphasis, or interest to a research paper, not to pad its length. Excess quoting of sources reduces the effectiveness of a paper because it suggests overdependence on other people's ideas.

   From page 108 of Perrin, Robert. Handbook for College Research. *New York: Houghton Mifflin Company, 1997.*

2. Write a proper paraphrase of the paragraph below according to the instructions in this chapter.

   College students appear to judge cheating as a matter of degree, with plagiarism—perhaps sharing work with a friend or lifting a sentence from an Internet page—as relatively minor, according to a 1999 study of beginning psychology students at a public university. The results, reported by G. A. U. Overbey and S. F. Guilding in "Student Perception of Plagiarism and the Evaluation of Assignments," Journal of Excellence in College Teaching, *1999(3), found that more than 70 percent of students said they should be able to resubmit a paper prepared for a previous course. Nearly 65 percent said they should have a chance to redo a paper, rather than receive a zero and be referred for additional campus sanctions, if an instructor catches some plagiarism in the work. Only 3 percent thought "plagiarism" should lead to discipline outside the classroom, while 19 percent said that submission of a purchased paper (a more egregious form of plagiarism, but plagiarism nonetheless) should be referred for student affairs action. Forty-one percent said a zero grade is appropriate for fully copied work. But another 30 percent said that students submitting work with some copied materials should get at least 50 percent credit for "effort."*

   From page 4 of "How Students View Plagiarism: Implications for Student Services." National On-Campus Report *30.5 (2002).*

3. If you are using InfoTrac College Edition in your course, access the following article in the database [*Hint:* conduct a "Title Search"]:

Petress, Kenneth C. "Academic dishonesty: a plague on our profession." Education 123.3 (2003): 624–27.

Write a brief summary of this essay (4–6 sentences). If you directly quote, remember to enclose these words in quotation marks.

4. Using your passcode, access the InfoTrac College Edition database and conduct a "Keyword" search for the phrase "plagiarism AND college." Scan the titles and abstracts of the articles that appear on the results page, and then write a brief paragraph (4–5 sentences) that summarizes common themes, attitudes, and viewpoints of these writers.

Index

Note: Entries followed by f indicate figures.

Credits

This page constitutes an extension of the copyright page. We have made every effort to trace the ownership of all copyrighted material and to secure permission from copyright holders. In the event of any question arising as to the use of any material, we will be pleased to make the necessary corrections in future printings. Thanks are due to the following authors, publishers, and agents for permission to use the material indicated.

Chapter 1

10   **Figure 1.1** Wikimedia Foundation Inc.

11   **Figure 1.2** Copyright © 2008 Microsoft Corporation.

12   **Figure 1.3** Courtesy of The Economist.

13   **Figure 1.4** From Frontline/WGBH Educational Foundation. Copyright © 2008 WGBH/Boston.

18   **Figure 1.5** Copyright 2009 EBSCO Publishing. All rights reserved.

Chapter 2

22   **Figure 2.1** Copyright 2008 Google Corporation. All rights reserved.

23   **Figure 2.2** Copyright 2008 Google Corporation. All rights reserved.

25   **Figure 2.3** Courtesy of Thomas Dowling/OhioLINK.

28   **Figure 2.4** Courtesy Ryerson University Library.

30   **Figure 2.6** Image published with permission of ProQuest LLC. Further reproduction is prohibited without permission. Research Library is produced by ProQuest LLC. Inquiries may be made to: ProQuest LLC, 789 Eisenhower Parkway, Ann Arbor, MI 48108 USA. Telephone (734) 761–4700; E-mail: info@proquest.com; Web-page: www .proquest.com.

34   **Figure 2.7** Courtesy of Library of Congress.

36   **Figure 2.8** Image published with permission of ProQuest LLC. Further reproduction is prohibited without permission. Research Library is produced by ProQuest LLC. Inquiries may be made to: ProQuest LLC, 789 Eisenhower Parkway, Ann Arbor, MI 48108 USA. Telephone (734) 761–4700; E-mail: info@proquest.com; Web-page: www .proquest.com.

37   **Figure 2.9** Image published with permission of ProQuest LLC. Further reproduction is prohibited without permission. Research Library is produced by ProQuest LLC. Inquiries may be made to: ProQuest LLC, 789 Eisenhower Parkway, Ann Arbor, MI 48108 USA. Telephone (734) 761–4700; E-mail: info@proquest.com; Web-page: www .proquest.com.

38   **Figure 2.10** Image published with permission of ProQuest LLC. Further reproduction is prohibited without permission. Research Library is produced by ProQuest LLC. Inquiries may be made to: ProQuest LLC, 789 Eisenhower Parkway, Ann Arbor, MI 48108 USA. Telephone (734) 761–4700; E-mail: info@proquest.com; Web-page: www.proquest.com.

Chapter 3 © 2008 by Consumers Union of U.S., Inc. Yonkers, NY 10703–1057, a nonprofit organization. Screen capture reprinted with permission for educational purposes only. No commercial use or reproduction permitted. www .ConsumerReports.org.

42 **Figure 3.1** Copyright 2009 EBSCO Publishing. All rights reserved.

44 **Figure 3.2** (top) Copyright 2009 EBSCO Publishing. All rights reserved.

44 **Figure 3.3** (bottom) Copyright 2009 EBSCO Publishing. All rights reserved.

46 **Figure 3.4A** Courtesy Ryerson University Library.

46 **Figure 3.4B** Courtesy Ryerson University Library.

47 **Figure 3.5** Copyright 1996–2007. Courtesy College Center for Library Automation (CCLA), Tallahassee, FL.

48 **Figure 3.6** Copyright 1996–2007. Courtesy College Center for Library Automation (CCLA), Tallahassee, FL.

51 **Figure 3.7** Courtesy of Stetson University Library and Sirsi Corporation.

52 **Figure 3.8** © 2008 by Consumers Union of U.S., Inc. Yonkers, NY 10703-1057, a nonprofit organization. Screen capture reprinted with permission for educational purposes only. No commercial use or reproduction permitted. www.ConsumerReports.org.

54 **Figure 3.9** CBC News.

54 **Figure 3.9** Photo of Roy Romanow: The Canadian Press (Jeff McIntosh).

55 **Figure 3.10** Copyright © Australian Museum, 2008. Reprinted with permission. http://www.amonline.net.au/herpetology/resources/reptiles_references.htm.

57 **Figure 3.11** Copyright 1996–2007. Courtesy College Center for Library Automation (CCLA), Tallahassee, FL.

58 Cornelis, Guy R, and Van Gijsegem, Frederique. "Assembly and Function of Type III Secretory Systems" Annual Review of Microbiology 54 (2000): 735–74. Academic Search Premier. EBSCOHost Seminole Community College Library. 3 Jan. 2006.

59 **Figure 3.12** Copyright 2009 EBSCO Publishing. All rights reserved.

61 **Figure 3.13** Copyright 1996–2007. Courtesy College Center for Library Automation (CCLA), Tallahassee, FL.

Chapter 4

67 **Figure 4.1** Copyright 2009 EBSCO Publishing. All rights reserved.

68 **Figure 4.2** Copyright 2007 LexisNexis, a division of Reed Elsevier Inc. All Rights Reserved. LexisNexis and the Knowledge Burst logo are registered trademarks of Reed Elsevier Properties Inc. and are used with the permission of LexisNexis.

72 **Figure 4.3** Courtesy Ryerson University Library.

74 **Figure 4.6** Copyright 2009 EBSCO Publishing. All rights reserved.

75 **Figure 4.7** Copyright 2009 EBSCO Publishing. All rights reserved.

Chapter 5

81 **Figure 5.1** Image published with permission of Ontario Council of University Libraries.

83 **Figure 5.2** Reproduced with permission of Yahoo! Inc. © 2007 by Yahoo! Inc. YAHOO! and the YAHOO! logo are trademarks of Yahoo! Inc.

84   **Figure 5.3** Copyright 2008 Google Corporation. All rights reserved.

85   **Figure 5.4** Reproduced with permission of Yahoo! Inc. © 2007 by Yahoo! Inc. YAHOO! and the YAHOO! logo are trademarks of Yahoo! Inc.

86   **Figure 5.5** Wikipedia® is a registered trademark of the Wikimedia Foundation Inc.

87   **Figure 5.6** Florida Museum of Natural History.

88   **Figure 5.7** Courtesy of Librarians' Internet Index.

91   **Figure 5.8** Reproduced with permission of Yahoo! Inc. © 2007 by Yahoo! Inc. YAHOO! and the YAHOO! logo are trademarks of Yahoo! Inc.

Chapter 6

102   **Figure 6.1** © Queens' Printer for Ontario, 2008. Reproduced with permission.

Documentation: APA Format: Austin's Turtle Page at http://www.austinturtlepage.com/.

Documentation: CSE Format: Courtesy JB Music http://www.jbmusic.ca; Creative Arts/Integrative Therapies Research Group <http://www.cait.fr.nf>. Dr. Carole-Lynne Le Navenec, RN, PhD, Associate Professor, Faculty of Nursing, PF 2260, University of Calgary, 2500 University Drive N.W., Calgary, Alberta, T2N 1N4, e-mail: cllenave@ucalgary.ca.